Due Return Date Date	Due Return Date Date

AN ECONOMY AT RISK

Does Anyone Care?

Judith Staley Brenneke, Editor
Rational Education Associates
and John Carroll University
Cleveland, Ohio

Francis W. Rushing, Series Editor
Ramsey Chair of Private Enterprise
Georgia State University

Sponsored by
Society of Economics Educators

1992

Georgia State University Business Press
College of Business Administration
Atlanta, Georgia

The Library of Congress Cataloging-in-Publication Data

An Economy at risk : does anyone care? / Judith Staley Brenneke,
  editor.
        p.   cm.
    Includes bibliographical references.
    ISBN 0-88406-248-1
        1. Economics—Study and teaching (Secondary)—United States.
    2. Economics—Study and teaching —United States. I. Brenneke,
    Judith Staley.
    HB74.8.E29 1992
    330'.071 ' 273—dc20   91-37340
                                                                CIP

Georgia State University Business Press
College of Business Administration
University Plaza
Atlanta, Georgia 30303-3093

©1992 Georgia State University

96 95 94 93 92   5 4 3 2 1

Georgia State University, a unit of the University System of Georgia,
is an equal educational opportunity institution and an equal
opportunity/affirmative action employer.

Printed in the United States of America.

Cover design by Patton H. McGinley, Jr.

/339059

AN ECONOMY AT RISK: DOES ANYONE CARE?

Table of Contents

PREFACE

On a hot summer day in 1988, twelve individuals deliberated the past, present, and future of their profession. Embodying a combined total of over two-hundred years of teaching, research, and program development experience in economics education, these members of the *Society of Economics Educators* were seeking a definitive answer to an old question, "Can a case be made for economics education at the pre-college level?" At the same time, they attempted to envision what economics skills and knowledge would be needed in the waning years of this century, and the impending years of the coming century.

An Economy at Risk is the four-phase project that emerged from that spirited summer afternoon.

- This book, *An Economy at Risk: Does Anyone Care?*, is an attempt to scrutinize the rationale for economics education.

- The accompanying monograph, *An Economy at Risk: The Case for Economics Education* presents the grounds for teaching pre-college economics identified through the papers in this volume.

However, these publications are merely the beginning of the process of exploring an economy at risk. Remaining are the essential steps of

- assessing what activities have been carried out during the past 30 years and appraisal of their success or failure; and

- developing a *Blueprint for Action on Economics Education in the 21st Century* designed to expand on past success in building for the future.

Realization of these first two volumes was made possible through partial funding from The National Federation for Independent Business, the NFIB Foundation, the Calvin K. Kazanjian Economics Foundation, the Center for Economic Education at

Purdue University, and the Bernard B. and Eugenia A. Ramsey Chair of Private Enterprise at Georgia State University. Considerable time and effort was contributed by members of the Society of Economics Educators, by Rational Education Associates, and by the Georgia State University Business Press.

This volume was designed to stimulate thought and discussion. If you actively agree or disagree with our findings -- if you begin examining your own efforts in economics education -- if you are angry or pleased -- we have succeeded.

Judith Staley Brenneke
Editor

Members of the
Society of Economics Educators

Judith Staley Brenneke
Rational Education Associates

Stephen Buckles
Joint Council on Economic
Education

Calvin A. Kent
U.S. Department of Energy,
Baylor University (on leave)

Marilyn Kourilsky
University of California, Los
Angeles

James B. O'Neill
University of Delaware

Francis W. Rushing
Georgia State University

Phillip Saunders
Indiana University

John C. Soper
John Carroll University

Robert J. Strom
Federal Reserve Bank of Kansas
City

George Vredeveld
University of Cincinnati

Michael J. Watts
Purdue University

Dennis J. Weidenaar
Purdue University

THE CASE FOR ECONOMICS EDUCATION

Judith Staley Brenneke

Although the American economic system has been called one of the wonders of the world, the continued success of this system is being questioned. Detractors suggest our economy is at risk when the next generation of entrepreneurs, workers, and consumers (today's high school students) displays misunderstandings and ignorance about the system. In 1986, the national norming of the *Test of Economic Literacy (TEL)* (Soper 1987) identified the following:

- Only **30%** know that low income results from the **lack of marketable skills**.

- In fact, **48%** think that high wages are a result of **minimum wage laws, government actions**, or **socially responsible business leaders**.

- Only **34%** can identify **profits** as revenues minus costs.

- **45%** realize that **government deficits** result when spending exceeds revenues.

- **17%** do not know who are hurt most by **inflation** (manufacturers, bondholders, borrowers, or farmers).

A significant market has grown up around the teaching of economics. School systems, colleges and universities, individual teachers, and governmental units are heavily involved in shaping the products of this industry. Millions of dollars a year are contributed by businesses, foundations, educational institutions, and governmental units to support the objectives of economic literacy.

However, in observing these efforts over the past several decades, we find that there are **questions that *should* have been answered -- *and were not*.** It is our goal through this

1

project to review those questions most commonly asked, and to finally provide some answers.

The Case For Economics Education

Why is it important that people learn about economics? (page 3)

What kind of economics is taught through economics education? (page 6)

Who determines what our children learn about the economy? (page 8)

What different behaviors will result from economics education? (page 11)

Who supports the teaching of economics at the pre-college level? (page 13)

Why is it important that people learn about economics?

The world of tomorrow will require much more of its citizens than the ability to read, write, and perform arithmetic functions. Tomorrow's citizens must be able to think, to analyze and assess, and to make decisions that will direct the agenda of our nation. Economics stands out among disciplines because it teaches theory, requires analysis, and blends the rigors of science with the necessities of human welfare. Economics grapples with the realities of change and requires the learner to adapt to new and dynamic phenomena. Economics should be taught, not as a substitute for other disciplines, but as a core discipline upon which others can draw, build and complement. An understanding of economics will provide the decision-making capabilities that will enable the United States to respond to this dynamically changing world -- and to further our progress into the future.

> **High-school graduates will be making economic choices all their lives, as breadwinners and consumers, and as citizens and voters. A wide range of people will bombard them with economic information and misinformation for their entire lives. They will need some capacity for critical judgment.** (Rushing 1992, 29)

The preceding quotation from James Tobin, 1981 Nobel Laureate, in a *Wall Street Journal* article, concisely summarizes the dual benefits of learning about economics -- individual benefit in making decisions as a worker, consumer, investor, or entrepreneur; *and* societal benefit in producing better citizens and voters. As Nobel prizewinner Paul Samuelson states, "All your life -- from cradle to grave and beyond -- you will run up against the brute truths of economics." (Ibid., 27)

These individual and societal roles also are perceived by the business community as reflected in a 1962 statement of the Committee for Economic Development:

3

> Our personal lives, no less than our public
> ones, require economic decisions. Re-
> sources, be they money, or time, or any of
> the other scarce things of life, must be allo-
> cated -- and reasoned allocation of resourc-
> es is the essential subject of economics.
> (O'Neill 1992, 19)

In fact, business recognizes its own self-interest benefits from
having an economically literate citizenry as described by Frederick
W. Wet, Jr., former president of Bethlehem Steel:

> **Economic Education, at all levels is one of
> the most important things we can do. It can
> decide the kind of economic and political
> environment we will be operating in for a
> long, long time to come. . . . The need was
> never greater; the opportunity never better.**
> (Ibid., 22)

The education establishment shares some of these same
interests. The National Council for the Social Studies asserts that
the "basic goal of social studies education is to prepare young
people to be humane, rational, participating citizens in a world
that is becoming increasingly interdependent." (Vredeveld 1992,
161.) Economics, as a social science discipline, identifies itself
with this citizenship goal. In addition, as early as 1933 Frederick
G. Nichols, known as the grandfather of business education,
stated:

> **There is need for greater understanding of
> those inexorable economic laws, the conse-
> quences of which, good or bad, none per-
> manently can escape. It is the obligation of
> business educators to see to it that their
> students leave them with a better under-
> standing of those economic laws in accor-
> dance with which business must be carried
> on and the ways in which these laws work
> for good or ill to mankind.** (Clow 1985, 4)

These arguments for economics education from the tangential disciplines of social studies and business education lead to a wider specification of the benefits of economics education: the "public goods" aspect of economics knowledge. If the study of economics confers *private* benefits to the learner (so that he or she, as a consequence, becomes a better consumer, worker, investor, or entrepreneur), then *the individual will be able to capture those benefits*. But, if the study of economics enables the learner to make better and more informed choices as a voter or other participant in our democratic system, then the individual does not capture all of the benefits. They spill over onto the larger society, conferring benefits on those who have *not* studied economics. As is well known to economists, such a situation leads to an underconsumption (or underinvestment) in economic literacy. The conclusion to this argument has been stated most eloquently by George Stigler, the 1982 Nobel laureate:

> **That the public does concern itself most frequently with economic questions -- is a true and persuasive reason for its possessing economic literacy. In the best of all worlds it might be most desirable to have musical or theological literacy, but in ours the public wants to talk about money. Although the public cannot have universal literacy, this is not reason for possessing no special knowledge at all. The public has chosen to speak and vote on economic problems so the only open question is how intelligently it speaks or votes.** (Rushing op. cit., 29)

Although the public goods argument for economics education (that the public as a whole will benefit from economic literacy) may be the strongest argument for including economics in K-12 education, it is the personal or private benefits that persuade individuals to *learn* economics.

Individuals may not perceive the benefit of learning economics so that they "become better voters and citizens." However, the influence of economics on individual career, consumption, and investment decisions can provide a strong private incentive for learning this subject.

5

What *kind* of economics is taught through economics education?

In spite of the general belief that economists can never agree on anything, most fundamental conceptual understandings are accepted as part of the core of economic theory. Included in these basic concepts are the fundamental concept of scarcity, which necessitates choices and places constraints on those choices; microeconomic concepts, examining individual markets and how they operate; macroeconomic concepts, analyzing the aggregate economy and attempts to stabilize it; and international concepts, addressing issues such as trade and payments between countries.

Disagreement often appears when these concepts are applied to specific situations and the determination of what economic policies might (or should) be undertaken.

Should economics describe what is -- or what should be?

Economics can provide the tools with which individuals can make decisions in a dynamic world. These concepts may be taught from a basis of what is called **"positive economics"** (an examination of what *is*), or from a basis of **"normative econom-ics"** (an examination of what *should be*). Armed with **positive** economic concepts, students can predict the results of various economic actions. Their predictions can be tested using scientific means. Students will be able to use these understandings in the future to alter their behavior, based on economic events, rather than merely sit in frustration and wonder, or respond inappropriately as economic events whirl around them.

If students are taught only **normative** propositions about "how the world *should* work," they will be limited in their analyses of future economic events. If students are taught merely that business *should* make a profit -- or that tariffs *should* be raised to protect U.S. jobs -- then they will not have been given the tools of analysis to decide for themselves the results of these actions. Unless students understand that profits are an economic cost of

6

doing business (and that without profits there is no incentive for the businessperson to continue providing a product or service), they will not fully appreciate the results of actions that limit profits (or that limit competition). If students are merely told that U.S. jobs *should* be protected from foreign competition, then they will not understand why imports *and* exports decline after a tariff or quota is imposed or why the prices they pay must rise.

Economics education programs must provide students with the positive economic understandings that will allow them to analyze what has occurred, to hypothesize what is occurring, and to predict what will occur in our dynamically changing society.

**Should we teach economics --
or an understanding of the business system --
or an understanding of consumer decision-making?**

An examination of the economy indicates there is a basic circular flow of interdependent activity between businesses and households (with additional flows to governments and the international sector). Concentrating exclusively on only one sector in this circular flow (limiting course content either to the business system *or* to consumer decision making) sacrifices an understanding of the basic interdependencies and how activities flow throughout the economy, or how spillover effects from policy decisions may impact both consumers and producers. Students may find it difficult to transfer these economic understandings to their multiple roles as producers, consumers, and voting citizens.

A course involving fundamental economic theory -- and the application of that theory to economic events in the past, present, and future -- provides students with the appropriate tools that can be used throughout their lives.

Should economics courses stress theory or application?

Similar to other sciences, economics is built on a theoretical basis that must be understood before it can be applied to specific situations. If students were given a math problem and told to solve it without any prior theory regarding addition, subtraction, multiplication, or division, they would be likely to fail in their attempts at finding a solution. To predict the results of an increased tariff, students must understand markets, incentives, competition, and comparative advantage as well as supply and demand. Unless they understand the applicable economic theory, students will not be able to predict the outcome of proposed economic policies or the impact of significant economic events.

Likewise, merely learning fundamental economic theory provides no guarantee that students may ever be able to use this theory to analyze economic events. Learning the law of demand -- as price rises the quantity demanded decreases -- may not provoke the interest of many students. However, understanding that increasing the price of oil will lower the quantity of oil demanded, that increasing the price of labor will decrease the number of workers hired, or that increasing the fee for public transportation will decrease the number of riders, provides students with a powerful tool with which to analyze economic decisions.

Economics courses should provide students with fundamental economic theory *and* assist them in applying that theory to economic events. Developing in students the skill to apply economic theory in examining situations and events encourages the greatest future use of these economic tools.

Who determines what our children learn about the economy?

What our children are learning about economics is influenced by a wide variety of individuals, organizations, and institutions. It is difficult to attribute a primary role in content determination to any one of the following influences; in fact, content is determined by a combination of all of them. The problem in dealing with these multiple influences on economics learning emerges when attempting to improve what is learned by students in the classroom. Do you revise the school district curriculum, exert pressure on the board of education or school administration as a special interest organization, campaign for state-wide mandates, provide

8

teaching materials or textbooks, or do you train the classroom teacher?

The current movement to reform education, in general, appears to encourage some activities, specifically:

- Recognition of the preeminent role of the teacher in influencing student learning.

- Involvement of the entire community in school reform, including colleges and universities as well as members of the business community.

In actuality, the activity (or combination of activities) undertaken inevitably depends on an analysis of the individual school district and its needs.

School district curricula

Most states require that school districts develop formal written curricula for the courses offered and that these curricula be revised after a set number of years. The process for revising curricula differs depending on the district: some districts centralize the revision under the direction of a curriculum director; others utilize teams of classroom teachers in the revision process; while others may adopt (or adapt) existing curricula developed outside the district.

Perhaps the most influential impact of this formal curriculum on what is taught in the classrooms is its use in selecting textbooks. If the district uses the curriculum writing process as an opportunity to define the desired content, then selection of a textbook that includes this desired content will carry the curriculum into the classroom. However, if the formal curriculum is developed outside the purview of the classroom teacher or the textbook selection process, then it is questionable whether that formal curriculum actually represents what is taught in the classroom.

Outside influences

Special interest groups may influence course content by providing teaching materials, speakers, seminars, graduate-credit classes for teachers, or other incentives. A recent innovation, of brief television programs designed specifically for the classroom, *Channel 1 - TV*, provides classroom technology as well as direct input into the classroom for paying commercial advertisers. School boards, economists, local business and labor organizations, professional education organizations, the media, part-time employers of students, not-for-profit organizations, and even parents all influence what our children learn about the economy.

State Mandates

An examination of state education mandates on economics education reveals varied content requirements. These mandates range from a *required* full-semester course, emphasizing positive economic analysis, to *recommendations* that both positive and normative economic concepts be taught at undefined times throughout the existing school curriculum. The orientation of the mandate depends to a large extent on the pressure group pushing for the mandate. Strong special interest group pressures for mandates may indicate related special interest bias within the mandate.

Economics education can mean different things to different groups. It is up to economics educators, funders, and the educational establishment to examine the suggested content to ascertain the type of economics being presented -- and to consistently encourage the teaching of positive economic theory applied to the analysis of past, current, and future situations.

Textbooks, materials, and projects

A major influence in terms of course content is the textbook used in the class as well as auxiliary teaching/learning materials. In fact, many busy teachers simply accept the textbook as the course curriculum. Since no single high school economics text has captured more than a quarter of the market, substantially influencing the content of the economics course through modifications of the texts is difficult. Auxiliary materials or programs such as *Mini-Society*, *The Capstone Course*, or *Applied Economics* may determine an additional portion of the content, while audiovisual and print materials may be inserted at the discretion of the teacher.

The teacher

Further analysis of influence on classroom content must bring us to the teacher as the gatekeeper of what will be learned in the classroom. He or she is the last line of defense against bad or weak economics content. If the teacher is well trained in economics, then he or she will be able to analyze new materials, suggestions, and content and utilize that content which is appropriate for the classroom. If the teacher is not trained in economics, then the content will depend on the text or on the most recent or most persuasive influence.

What different behaviors will result from economics education?

In a school curriculum that is already full and in a school day that is already limited in time, one must question why economics is more important than additional time spent on reading, writing, or math skills (or time spent on literature, music, or art). One response might be to quote Herbert Stein, former Chairman of the Council of Economic Advisers:

> **There's a compelling reason for learning about economics which I tell my students. Economics is a large part of life in this country. If you read the daily newspaper, a large proportion of the stories in the paper are about economics. They're about economic policy, and they're about the behavior of the economy. To live in this country and not understand all this is just to miss a good deal of the excitement of being here.** (Ibid., 30)

Another criterion for justification is the changed behavior of the students after learning economics.

Quantitative evidence is available on the differing understandings of students at various grade levels. We have examined (1) what students are capable of understanding; (2) what they *do*, in fact, know; and (3) what they *do not* know, based on recent evidence from test development and norming at the elementary, middle school, and high school levels. However, this does not directly tell us how economics will influence the behavior of these students as producers, consumers, or as voting citizens.

We *do* know that an understanding of the underlying economics will increase consumers' satisfaction with the decisions they have made. (Kourilsky 1992, 157) We can assert that producers make more satisfactory decisions after considering the economics of the situation. However, we *do not* have any solid evidence that an understanding of economics will improve an individual's societal or citizenship role.

We cannot assume that because a person knows economics he or she will necessarily behave in a way that is better for society. In some cases economics knowledge is clearly in the best interest of society. Many groups promote their own self-interest and have become very good at stating their appeal in terms that are seemingly consistent with social welfare. The economically literate individual will accept or reject these comments after evaluating the best interest for society as a whole. However, the person who is economically literate is not necessarily more likely to vote for something that is in society's interest if the policy does not promote his or her own self-interest. It is possible that the dual purposes of economics understanding -- what is good for the individual and what is good for society -- will conflict with one another.

Close examination of what students now know, will assist us in determining how their behavior might be altered by learning more economics. As Nobel laureate Paul Samuelson states:

> **As a voter, you will have to make decisions on issues -- inflation, unemployment or protectionism -- that just can't be under-**

stood until you've mastered the rudiments of this subject.

Earning your lifetime income involves economics. So does spending that income as a consumer. In the important task of saving and investing -- the prudent handling of the nest egg that won't handle itself -- economics won't guarantee to make you a genius. But without economics the dice are simply loaded against you. (Rushing op cit., 27)

Who supports the teaching of economics at the pre-college level?

The business community has traditionally been the primary supporter of economics education. In his 1967 testimony before the Sub-Committee on Economic Progress, Alfred C. Neal, president of the Committee for Economic Development, suggested that the motivation for business support reflected both *self-interest* and *philosophy.*

[Self interest] is simply that business wants to operate at a profit and wants the public to understand that profit . . . is a good measure of business performance in the public interest. Freedom from too much regulation, taxation or pressure is essential to attaining satisfactory profits. . . .

The philosophical argument for economics advanced by many businessmen is based upon the inseparability of political and economic freedom. Just as political freedom depends on the right of the citizen to have a voice in the affairs of government. . . .

So economic freedom depends upon decentralization of economic power and particularly upon the

free choice of millions of economic decision makers.
(O'Neil op cit., 21)

Economics education at the pre-college level is advocated by a variety of educational organizations representing teachers of social studies, business, home economics, and vocational programs. The American Economic Association Committee on Economic Education has played an influential role in involving professional economists in this area. And, if involvement in programs across the country and an increase in the economics contained within published textbooks is an indication, economics in the pre-college curriculum is increasingly accepted by classroom teachers from kindergarten through twelfth grade. The expansion in the number of states mandating some type of economics education reflects both the increased support for this subject from educators, *and* increased pressure by outside constituencies (such as business, labor, or higher education).

Perhaps the best indication of support for economics education is the growth of the number of organizations in the industry. Although a review of these organizations will identify diverse rationales, objectives, and strategies, all have identified supporters who champion positions that may be summarized under the following categories:

1. Provide understandings that are essential for success in the marketplace.

2. Create a better awareness and understanding of the American economy and the free enterprise system.

3. Provide an understanding of economics issues so voters can make more intelligent decisions.

4. Demonstrate the relationship between economic and political liberty.

5. Show that economic freedom is an essential part of a moral and just society.

6. Enhance the capacity for rational decision making. (Kent and Weidenaar 1992, 86)

The issue is not *if* there is support for economics education. The issue is the determination of the optimal goals for economics education and identification of the organizations that are accomplishing those goals effectively and efficiently. Meanwhile, the market for economics education organizations is quite active.

The Case for Economics Education: A Conclusion

Although this research project began with a question, *Is there a case for economics education?*. It is concluding with a statement, *Yes, there IS a case for economics education*. We live in a dynamically changing world. A world where Eastern Europe is in ferment attempting to define a new political and, especially, *economic* order. This is a world where we increasingly rely on other countries to buy our goods and services and to provide goods and services for us to buy, and where financial capital is available in a variety of languages. Our world is a society that continually attempts to find new and more satisfactory answers to old social and economic problems.

The case for teaching economics may simply be that economics teaches best the rational thinking process. No other subject creates a more vivid understanding of trade-offs -- the costs and benefits of alternative choices. No other subject to which students will be exposed better equips them for evaluating alternative courses of action or inaction.

The content of the economics programs in the schools should be based in the science of economics and applied to issues and situations as often as possible. Through this process children will not only learn the basic tools they will need but will also learn when and how these tools can be used. Consistent application of the basic concepts will increase their transferability to new issues in the future.

Now that the *Case for Economics Education* has been established, it is incumbent upon everyone involved that optimal ways of helping students gain this economic literacy be identified.

The baseline data on evaluation of student understanding that are now available may offer a starting point by which future economics education efforts may be assessed. This, in turn, could encourage an assessment of organizations offering these economics education programs. Above all, innovative and effective programs must continue to be developed to meet the needs of this *economy that is at risk.*

References

Clow, John E. ed. 1987. *Economics in the Business Curriculum*. second edition. New York: Joint Council on Economic Education.

Kent, Calvin A. and Dennis Weidenaar. 1992. "Goals, Rationale, and Strategies Employed by Economics Education Organizations: A Summary and Analysis." *An Economy at Risk: Does Anyone Care?* Atlanta, Georgia: Georgia State University Business Press.

Kourilsky, Marilyn. 1992. "Economics Education and Satisfaction with Family Decision-Making." *An Economy at Risk: Does Anyone Care?* Atlanta, Georgia: Georgia State University Business Press.

O'Neill, James B. 1992. "A Brief History of the Rationale for Economics Education." *An Economy at Risk: Does Anyone Care?* Atlanta, Georgia: Georgia State University Business Press.

Rushing, Francis W. 1992. "The Position of Distinguished Economists on Economics Education." *An Economy at Risk: Does Anyone Care?* Atlanta, Georgia: Georgia State University Business Press.

Soper, John C. and William Walstad. 1987. *Test of Economic Literacy*. New York: Joint Council on Economic Education.

Vredeveld, George M. 1992. "Why Teach the Social Studies: A Look at the Rationale for Individual Disciplines." *An Economy at Risk: Does Anyone Care?* Atlanta, Georgia: Georgia State University Business Press.

A BRIEF HISTORY OF THE RATIONALE FOR ECONOMICS EDUCATION

James B. O'Neill

The economic failure of the 1930s, followed by economic stimulation of World War II, caused many business leaders to have feelings of uncertainty about the economy as it shifted to peace-time objectives. They were painfully aware of the economic problems associated with the thirties and believed one strategy to avoid a future economic calamity, such as the depression of the previous decade, was through increased economic education. As the U.S. economy shifted to peacetime objectives, their concerns about the general public's lack of knowledge about economics were the primary impetus to the formation of the Committee for Economic Development (CED). This organization was created to assist the citizenry in raising the level of economic understanding. After discussing and reflecting on the role of economics educa-tion, the CED released the following policy statement:

> We believe the need for economic knowledge is growing rapidly. We fear that this need is not widely enough recognized, nor its implication adequately understood.
>
> The complexity of our economic affairs grows with our institutions. Businesses are bigger, so are labor unions, so are our local, state and Federal governments. All of these institutions require eco-nomic decision making and in a democracy all of us, to a large extent, must be our own economists.
>
> Our personal lives, no less than our public ones, require economic decisions. Resources, be they money, or time, or any of the other scarce things of life, must be allocated -- and reasoned allocation of resources is the essential subject of economics.
>
> Such knowledge, we believe, may contribute to the happiness of the new generation of adults. It

**will certainly make them more efficient and more
effective in their private lives and as citizens. It
would be tragic, we believe, to graduate still another
generation of Americans without the basic analytical
tools of economic reasoning.** (CED 1962, 8)

During this transition period, members of the business community were willing to support economics education because they
believed "economic literacy was vital to the survival of the American Society." (1962, 9) The compelling reason for this support of
economics education was expressed by Alfred C. Neal, president
of the CED, in 1967 in testimony before the Sub-Committee on
Economic Progress. He divided the underlying rationale for
business support for economics education into *self-interest*
and *philosophical* positions. The *self-interest* portion "is
simply that business wants to operate at a profit and wants the
public to understand that profit . . . is a good measure of business
performance in the public interest. Freedom from too much
regulation, taxation or pressure is essential to attaining satisfactory profits."

Whereas, he continued, "the philosophical argument for
economics advanced by many businessmen is based upon the
inseparability of political and economic freedom. Just as political
freedom depends on the right of the citizen to have a voice in the
affairs of government . . . so economic freedom depends upon
decentralization of economic power and particularly upon the free
choice of millions of economic decision makers." (1967, 237)

The CED provided the vehicle for business to have a rationale
to support economics education. Many of the economics education programs of the 1950s were directed toward employee
education with limited focus on teacher education. In the early
1960s, several early pioneers in economics education believed the
goal of economic literacy should also include increased teacher
education. They believed this educational process should concentrate on two important variables, teacher training as well as the
improvement in the quantity and quality of materials. In 1962
Lewis Wagner indicated the achievement of quality economics
education programs was not one-dimensional; in addition to
training teachers, materials must be made available to assist the
teacher. His study indicated the importance of not only develop-

ing good materials but also of increasing the ability of the teacher to relate materials to their students. He stated, "a well-constructed resource unit, however, necessitates considerable translation by the teacher." (Wagner 1962, 101)

The importance of improving the status of economics education in the schools has been an important objective of the business community since the early pioneering efforts in the 1950s and 1960s. Some business leaders naively assumed that economics education was merely the modification of values; however, the Business Roundtable in its *1974 Survey* emphasized the importance of a strong base of economics knowledge in the following statement:

> **There is a strong correlation between people's attitude toward business and the amount of correct economic information they have. The higher they score on a test of basic economics the more favorable they look at business organizations as a group.** (Virginia Council on Economic Education 1978, 1)

Business leaders have continued to take a strong position regarding the importance of economics education. Often their support is expressed in terms of how economics may correlate to other disciplines or areas of interest. Richard Heckert, retired Chairman of the Board, E.I. duPont de Nemours, emphasized the importance of economic understanding in the context of government. He raised the question:

> **How can we run a populist democracy, a market economy, a private enterprise system, unless young people understand basic economic principles, laws, and the trade-offs involved in making social decisions? They should have some understanding of why we picked the economic system we have.** (Joint Council on Economic Education 1986, front cover)

Since World War II the steel industry has confronted a variety of obstacles, some self-created with others initiated through government interference. The ever-changing position of government may have led the former president of Bethlehem Steel

Corporation, Frederic W. West, Jr., to make a strong appeal for economics education by stating:

> Economic education, at all levels, is one of the most important things we can do. It can decide the kind of economic and political environment we will be operating in for a long, long time to come . . . where do we go from here with economic education? The answer, in my opinion, is that we've got to knuckle down and get the story across. The need was never greater; the opportunity never better. (Joint Council on Economic Education, 1977, 10)

The role of technology in all aspects of the economy is receiving increased attention as we move into the highly sophisticated economy of the next century. The late James E. Olson, chairman, American Telephone & Telegraph, indicated in the following quote that improved technology without economics education would short-circuit our future growth:

> We in business are making huge investments in new technology to improve our productivity, to manage operations, to meet competition from abroad. If we don't make a similar investment in the economic education of our young people -- who will be running that technology in the future -- our capital investments may go for naught. (Joint Council on Economic Education, 1986, front cover)

Both corporations and foundations continue to make large investments in economics education. One of the more influential foundations, The Pew Charitable Trusts, indicated their strong concern for economics education in their most recent annual report:

> Understanding how our economic system works and the individual's role within it is an important obligation of American citizenship. Few people, however, have more than a superficial grasp of the laws that govern our free enterprise system, with much of this understanding gained experientially through working in the marketplace. (The Pew Charitable Trusts 1988, 160)

Although many questions have been raised regarding the benefits of economics education, businesses have continued to support the economics education movement. Continuing support in economics education can best be explained by Richard E. Heckert. He states, "Without economic understanding throughout the community, the leaders cannot make or communicate sensible policy and the public will not be persuaded to make the sacrifices necessary to keep our economy healthy and our society free." (Delaware Council on Economic Education 1986, 1)

As more groups claim to offer economics education programs, it becomes increasingly important for organizations asking for financial support for economics education to have a clear focus and precise objectives. Some questions potential contributors may ask are:

- What returns have we received from our investment in economics education?

- What evidence do we have that teachers are being trained rather than entertained?

- What evidence do we have that students are learning economics?

- Is there an optimal mix -- public/private -- support for economics education?

Although there are, no doubt many others, the foregoing questions reflect concerns on the future status and direction of economics education. As we start the decade of the 1990s, the leaders in economics education must address these questions, as well as others, if continued financial support is expected.

References

Baker, G. Derwood. 1949. "Education for Economic Understanding." New York: Joint Council on Economic Education.

Committee for Economic Development. 1985. "Building Consensus on the Crucial Issues." *Annual Report.*

Committee for Economic Development. 1962. *Economic Literacy for Americans.*

Delaware Council on Economic Education. 1986. "Economic Education in the Delaware Schools."

First National City Bank. 1962. "Economics for the Thinking Citizen: A Report on Economic Education for Employees."

Frankel, M.L. 1980. "The Joint Council on Economic Education, Highlights of its Development 1949-1980." preliminary report.

Hearings before the Subcommittee on Economic Progress of the Joint Economic Committee. 1967. Volume II. Washington, D.C.: U.S. Government Printing Office.

Joint Council on Economic Education. 1977. *Annual Report.*

Joint Council on Economic Education. 1985-86. *Annual Report.*

Joint Council on Economic Education. 1959. *Education for the Economic Challenges of Tomorrow.*

The Pew Charitable Trusts. 1988. *Annual Report.*

Virginia Council on Economic Education. 1978. *Annual Report.*

Wagner, Lewis E. 1962. "Progress in Closing the Materials Gap in Economic Education." *The Bulletin.* Volume 46.

THE POSITION OF DISTINGUISHED ECONOMISTS ON ECONOMIC EDUCATION

Francis W. Rushing

Why should economics be taught to young Americans? How often this question is asked of those of us involved in economics education. Although the answer seems to be intuitively obvious, one does look for a case for teaching economics among the writings of famous economists. Therefore, it seemed like a worthy task to search the literature and published statements of noted economists to see why *they* believe economics should be taught in elementary and secondary schools. This paper reports on an investigation into a variety of sources to discover the position of distinguished economists on economics education. The hypothesis driving this search was that those individuals most recognized by the discipline have surely laid a foundation for a rationale for teaching the discipline.

Nobel Prize in Economic Science Recipients

The Prize in Economic Science in Memory of Alfred Nobel was established in 1968 by a donation of the Bank of Sweden to the Nobel Foundation. The memorial prize follows the same principal rules as the Nobel Prize awarded in the other disciplines by the Royal Swedish Academy of Sciences. What is noteworthy about the addition of economic sciences to the other sciences is that it is the first new science to be added to the Nobel Prize in its 89 years of existence. According to correspondence with the Nobel Foundation (Lemmel 1987), the Board of Directors of the Foundation receives numerous requests for expansion of the prizes awarded, including suggestions in the areas of mathematics, environment, engineering, music, and ballet. The Board of Directors, however, has refused to expand the award except for economics. Their reasoning for including economics was that Alfred Nobel played an important role in business and finance and, therefore, a prize in economics was related to his life. Furthermore, there was strong support for initiating an economics prize from the Bank of Sweden and from leading Swedish economists, particularly Gunnar Myrdal (a Nobel Prize winner in 1974). Certainly the expansion of the Nobel prizes to include economics raised the stature of this discipline, although there is no evidence that the rationale for the new prize was based on any need to have people learn economics but rather was related to the life of Alfred Nobel.

Given the new status of economics among the sciences, a review of the acceptance speeches of the prize winners was undertaken. Although not all of the acceptance speeches were reviewed, those that were studied contained no specific references to a desire or need to teach economics either as a science or as a life skill. Undaunted, we concluded that the absence of published pronouncements at the Nobel Prize ceremonies does not necessarily mean that the prizewinners would not be strong advocates for economics education, but only that they did not take that opportunity to express this view.

American Economic Association Presidents

A second source, the presidential addresses of the presidents of the American Economic Association, was reviewed in search for support for economics education. These are published annually in the *American Economic Review*, and looking back over the last twenty years one does not find the presidents discussing economics education in their presidential addresses. Like the Nobel prizewinners (and sometimes these are one and the same people), the presidents of the association tended to explore with their fellow economists issues either related to economic theory or to matters of economic policy. What economist could pass up the opportunity with such distinguished audiences to press points within the discipline on which many hours of research and analysis were based!

The Advocates of Economic Literacy -- A Sampler

Where, then, might such distinguished economists expound on their advocacy of economics education? Several appropriate vehicles were uncovered -- books, journals, newspapers, and magazines. For instance, Nobel prizewinner and past president of the American Economic Association Paul Samuelson took the opportunity in the foreword to the twelfth edition of his textbook, *Economics*, to make an eloquent case for economics education of our students:

> **Still, we have come to realize, there is one overriding reason for needing to study economics.**
>
> **All your life -- from cradle to grave and beyond -- you will run up against the brute truths of economics. As a voter, you will have to make decisions on issues -- inflation, unemployment or protectionism -- that just can't be understood until you've mastered the rudiments of this subject.**
>
> **Earning your lifetime income involves economics. So does spending that income as a consumer. In the important task of saving and investing -- the prudent handling of the nest egg that won't handle itself -- economics won't guarantee to make you a genius. But without economics the dice are simply loaded against you. (Samuelson and Nordhaus 1985)**

Professor Samuelson also had periodic opportunities in his musings in *Newsweek* to touch on the value of economics within the educational setting. As he is quoted in a collection of these articles:

> **Economics used to be a dry subject that told you what you couldn't do. From a scholar's viewpoint that was never very good political economy in the first place. Readers of this generation are luckier than we used to be in my time. You can go beyond the quantity of economic life to its quality -- beyond**

gross national product to net economic welfare.
You can examine unflinchingly the flaws in the system as well as its merits. You can discover where
conventional wisdoms need to be junked, and best
of all, where new research can add to our knowledge. (Samuelson 1983)

Dr. Samuelson, as is obvious from these quotes, believed that
all individuals should have sufficient understanding of economics
to analyze many of the economic situations which they face and
to discuss the data which they read.

More recently, Paul Samuelson published his reflections on
economics education and the rationale for teaching it in a spring
1987 issue of the *Journal of Economic Education* devoted to
the scope of economics and what should be taught. In this article
he reflects as follows:

I shall not pretend to preach on high school economics. In my day at Hyde Park High School in
Chicago, the subject was not even taught. My first
teacher at the University of Chicago, Aaron Director,
was just as pleased. Jesuits like to work with virgin-
al material, and in those pre-Galbraith days I was
putty in Director's no-nonsense hands.

From what I hear in the senior common rooms,
things have not changed all that much. College
instructors go whole hours not brooding over what
is taught by way of high school economics, and
most would like to keep that terrain a curricular
vacuum.

However, economic education is too serious a
business to be left to university professors. There
are still millions of people who will never get to
college. And it could be the case -- although I
would not bet on it -- that in the tender years of
adolescence, the human brain is in an especially
flexible and receptive state for learning to speak
Hungarian or learning about present discounted

values and foreign-trade multipliers. (Samuelson 1987, 101)

Other Nobel laureates and past presidents of the AEA have taken their turn in print, both in the media and in journals, to state their views on a rationale for economics education. James Tobin, 1981 Nobel laureate, in a *Wall Street Journal* article stated:

> The case for economic literacy is obvious. High-school graduates will be making economic choices all their lives, as breadwinners and consumers, and as citizens and voters. A wide range of people will bombard them with economic information and misinformation for their entire lives. They will need some capacity for critical judgement. They will need it whether or not they go on to college. (Tobin 1986)

The Tobin quote seems particularly relevant for the case for economics education being discussed in this volume. He seems to argue that, as economists, what we have to say has relevance even to those who do not continue from elementary and secondary education to university classrooms. It seems to imply there is certain fundamental knowledge that all citizens need in order to grapple with their every day lives and to dissect and digest a constant stream of economic data -- and propaganda -- coming from local, state, and national organizations and elected officials.

The 1982 Nobel laureate, George Stigler, expressed his views on the case, if any, for economics education in a 1970 *Journal of Economic Education* article. To take only one paragraph from that journal, Dr. Stigler says:

> Yet this last point -- that the public does concern itself most frequently with economic questions -- is a true and persuasive reason for its possessing economic literacy. In the best of all worlds it might be most desirable to have musical or theological literacy, but in ours the public wants to talk about money. Although the public cannot have universal literacy, this is not reason for possessing no special knowledge at all. The public has chosen to speak and vote on economic problems so the only open

question is how intelligently it speaks or votes. (Stigler 1970, 82)

One can turn to economists who, though not Nobel prizewinners, are prominent economists in positions of public trust such as Herbert Stein, former Chairman of the Council of Economic Advisers:

> There's a compelling reason for learning about economics which I tell my students. Economics is a large part of life in this country. If you read the daily newspaper, a large proportion of the stories in the paper are about economics. They're about economic policy, and they're about the behavior of the economy. To live in this country and not understand all this is just to miss a good deal of the excitement of being here. It's like living in Pittsburgh and not understanding football. You are missing part of the life of your times, and I think that's too bad.
>
> I don't buy the idea that a person will only feel motivated to learn about economics if there's some dollar and cents payoff for him. To go back to my other example about football: If you can understand the process by which the professional football play-offs operate -- how teams get into the play-offs -- you know that is a terribly complicated set of calculations. But a lot of people sitting around in bars drinking beer understand that perfectly. Now there's no money in it for any of them, but it's interesting to them. And so I think the problem is to make economics sufficiently interesting. (1989)

Professor Stein makes a common sense argument, an example of not only why economics ought to be taught but also suggesting that it must be taught in a manner that will make it of interest to the potential learner. This is certainly a challenge to economic educators and suggests that if we have an opportunity to teach economics, we certainly should not blow that opportunity by doing it in a dry and uninteresting fashion. (How often have you heard students gasping as they exited the classroom that they just had the dullest experience of their lives?)

Leonard Silk, like Stein, seems to make a short but potent statement for teaching economics:

> **Anyone who meddles in economic issues becomes an economist of sorts. A generation ago, James Thurber and E.B. White asked, "Is Sex necessary?" Masters and Johnson have answered, "Nonsex is a form of sex." Noneconomics is a form of economics. Economics is necessary.** (Silk 1986)

Paul Heyne in his text, *The Economic Way of Thinking*, certainly conveys one idea that most economists have as to why we commit ourselves to teaching economics. His comments give us his perspective of the economics educators' special contribution:

> **The economic way of thinking employs such concepts as demand, opportunity cost, marginal effects and comparative advantage to order familiar phenomena. The economist knows very little about the real world that is not better known by business executives, artisans, engineers, and others who make things happen. What economists do know is how things fit together. The concepts of economics enable us to make better sense out of what we observe, to think more consistently and coherently about a wide range of interrelated phenomena.** (Heyne 1983, 453)

Then what we do have, after surveying Nobel laureates, American Economic Association presidents, and a perusal of the popular press? I think what we have discovered is at least the embryo of what we hoped would be there. Some who are among the distinguished in the profession have indeed nodded to the importance of economics education. They have cooperated with committees of their peers in looking at the scope and sequence for economics instruction. They have served on various task forces to support programs and activities such as those undertaken by the Joint Council on Economic Education in cooperation with the American Economic Association. These scholars have written for and published in the *Journal of Economic Education*, and in doing so have given importance to economics education and thereby given credibility to those who have devoted at least part of their professional activities to economics education for our pre-college students. It would seem appropriate to conclude with one last quote by Richard Cyert in a 1984 article:

> **We can have a society that is humane and an economy that is productive and dynamic if people in the society understand the system and behave rationally. That is why I feel intensely about the value of economic education. I also feel as strongly about the obligation universities and economists have to work with the elementary and secondary schools to help improve that understanding. (Cyert 1984, 264)**

References

Cyert, Richard. 1984. "Economic Education in Our Schools: A Renewed Mission." *Journal of Economic Education*. 15 (Fall).

Heyne, Paul. 1983. *The Economic Way of Thinking*. 4th ed. Chicago: SRA.

Lemmel, Birgitta. 1987. 20 May letter from Information Secretary, Nobelstiftelsen.

Samuelson, Paul A. 1983. "Preface to *Economics from the Heart: A Samuelson Sampler*." ed. Maryann O. Keating. New York: Harcourt Brace.

_____. 1987. "How Economics Has Changed." *Journal of Economic Education*. 18 (Spring).

_____ and William D. Nordhaus. 1985. *Economics*. 12th ed. New York: Harcourt Brace.

Silk, Leonard. 1986. *Economics in Plain English*. rev. ed. New York: Simon & Schuster.

Stein, Herbert. 1989. December personal interview quoting from *What Makes America Run.* 1981 booklet. Cleveland, Ohio: Standard Oil Company (Ohio).

Stigler, George. 1970. "The Case, if any, for Economic Education." *Journal of Economic Education*.

Tobin, James. 1986. "Economic Literacy Isn't a Marginal Investment." *Wall Street Journal*. (Wednesday, 9 July).

OFFICIAL POSITION OF THE AMERICAN ECONOMIC ASSOCIATION ON ECONOMICS EDUCATION

Phillip Saunders

As A. W. Coats pointed out in his 1985 article on "The American Economic Association and the Economics Profession," the American Economic Association (AEA) rarely takes an official position on anything. The Association's Certificate of Incorporation, which was printed in the December 1989 *American Economic Review*, (79 (6), ix) lists its purposes as:

1.   The encouragement of economic research.

2.   The issue of publications on economic subjects.

3.   The encouragement of perfect freedom of economic discussion. The Association as such will take no partisan attitude, nor will it commit its members to any position on practical economic questions.

The Association's three journals also contain the following disclaimers:

The American Economic Review: "No responsibility for the views expressed by authors in this *Review* is assumed by the editors or the publishers, The American Economic Association."

The Journal of Economic Literature: "No responsibility for the views expressed by authors and reviewers in the *Journal of Economic Literature* is assumed by the editors or by the publisher, the American Economic Association."

The Journal of Economic Perspectives: "No responsibility for the views expressed by the authors in this journal is assumed by the editors or by the American Economic Association."

Official certification or accreditation of individuals, courses, or programs is sometimes undertaken by professional associations in other disciplines; however, the AEA has consistently avoided this practice. Despite the lack of official endorsements, however, A. W. Coats has noted:

> **From its inception the AEA has demonstrated an intermittent interest in the improvement of economics teaching both at the high school and the college level, and of course some of its publication activities have been designed to raise the level of the general public's knowledge of economic affairs. . . . In 1965 a fruitful link was established with the Joint Council on Economic Education, which has enabled the Association to exert a considerable influence in the field through its representatives on the council without committing the Association as a body.** (1985, 1720)

A reading of the *American Economic Review Papers and Proceedings* volumes indicates that the AEA's link with the Joint Council on Economic Education (JCEE) began even before the 1965 date given by Coats. It appears that there have been at least six key milestones in the evolution of the AEA's current position in economic education:

- The appointment of a Committee on Undergraduate Teaching of Economics and the Training of Economists in 1944.

- The appointment of an Ad Hoc Committee on Graduate Training in Economics in 1950.

- The appointment of an Ad Hoc Committee on Economics in Teacher Education in 1952.

- The appointment of the first standing Committee on Economic Education in 1955.

- The appointment of a National Task Force on Economic Education in 1960.

- The appointment of the present standing Committee on Economic Education in 1964.

After a brief reference to the AEA's early interest in the teaching of economics, this paper will discuss each of these six developments. In tracing the evolution of the AEA's policy, I will quote from selected minutes of the Association's Executive Committee meetings and from reports of various AEA committees that have been published in the *Papers and Proceedings* volumes of *The American Economic Review (AER)*. In citing these quotations I will simply note the year and the pages (e.g. 1945, 485) without a full-scale citation appearing in the References section of this paper. It should be noted that the date of the *Papers and Proceedings* is one year later than the activities reported. That is, the 1945 *Papers and Proceedings* reports on activities during 1944, for example.

For those who would like to pursue individual committee reports in more detail than provided by the excerpts in this paper, Appendix I lists the thirty-nine reports that have appeared in the *AER, Papers and Proceedings* since 1950, showing the year, volume number, title, authors, and page numbers of the reports.

Appendix II lists the papers and discussions that have been presented at the thirty-four annual meetings of the AEA that have included sessions on economic education topics since 1950. This Appendix shows individual authors and discussants as well as page numbers in the appropriate volumes of the *AER, Papers and Proceedings*.

The story revealed in this paper is one of the evolution of an increasingly activist and project-oriented AEA policy that has involved a significant number of professional economists in a wide variety of activities. None of these activities have committed the Association as such on questions of what to teach or how to teach it at any level of economics instruction, but many have involved outstanding leaders of the profession in ways that have led to increasing status and prestige for those economists who have chosen to specialize in this area. The work and efforts of two key people, Ben W. Lewis and G. L. Bach, will be shown to have played the major roles in providing the leadership that has led to the evolution of the AEA's current policy.

Early Interest
in Economics Education

Laurence L. Leamer's article on "A Brief History of Economics and General Education" was published, along with the reports of the 1944 AEA Committee on the Undergraduate Teaching of Economics and the Training of Economists, in a special 226-page supplement to the December 1950, *AER*. This supplement was edited by the committee chairman, Horace Taylor of Columbia University, and Leamer's article indicates that between 1886 and 1944 the AEA devoted some time at fourteen of its annual meetings during this fifty-nine year period to roundtable discussions on the problems of general economic education. Three of these fourteen roundtables were specifically devoted to economics and the secondary schools -- in 1895, 1918, and 1921. Leamer's article presents a very comprehensive description and analysis of materials published on the teaching of economics up to 1950, and it is full of interesting observations and insights that summarize his lengthy bibliography that appeared in the same volume. (1950a and 1950b). Following the publication of the 1950 special supplement, some "Divergent Views of Members of the Subcommittee on Teaching the Elementary Course in Economics" were published in the June issue of the *AER* in the following year (Hewett 1951), and this particular subcommittee report served as the basis of a roundtable discussion at the December 1950, AEA meetings.

Activities and Recommendations
of the Taylor Committee

The AEA Committee on the Undergraduate Teaching of Economics and the Training of Economists grew out of discussions and correspondence initiated by President Albert B. Wolfe in 1943, and it was officially authorized at an AEA Executive Committee meeting on 7 April, 1944. Professor Horace Taylor of Columbia was made chairman of a five-person "parent" committee "to consider possible improvements in undergraduate teaching of economics and in the training of economists with primary reference to the long-run postwar period." (1945, 485)

Despite this rather strong orientation toward college and graduate-level economics, one of the parent committee's eleven subcommittees was appointed in the area of "The Teaching of Economics in the Schools," with S. Howard Patterson of the University of Pennsylvania as the subcommittee chairman. This subcommittee was soon so overwhelmed by the magnitude of the task confronting it, however, that it, along with two other subcommittees, did not issue a report when the findings of the Taylor Committee were published in 1950. The preface to the December 1950 *AER* supplement, however, contains this paragraph:

This has been conspicuously the most difficult of our several assignments. . . . As early as 1945, it was recognized that this group should not attempt a formal report, but should devote itself to learning something about the complexities and difficulties of general education in economics as carried on in the secondary schools. Chairman S. Howard Patterson, and also the secretary of the Committee, have devoted much study to this area. They also have formed a number of contacts with other associations and with official bodies with a view to the organization of a study by the National Council for the Social Studies, under the auspices of the AEA and other interested bodies, of the entire area that has come to be known as the social studies. The subcommittee's proposals to this end were included in the recommendations submitted with our report of December 1949. As this is written, the Executive Committee has not yet acted on these recommendations. Against the recommendations, it may be argued that this is a problem of specialists in pedagogy, rather than for economists and other social scientists. The rejoinder of the subcommittee is that, in the absence of the proposed study, it is difficult to back up this argument with convincing evidence. (December 1950, 40:5, Part 2, xi)

39

The Committee recommendations just referred to were worded as follows:

1. That we be authorized to publish our reports in the way described.

2. That a standing committee on eduction in economics, to carry on general activities similar to those of this Committee and any others that the proposed committee or the Executive Committee may deem desirable, be established.

3. That a committee be appointed to study and report on graduate training in economics, the report to consider both the development of scholarly techniques and capacities and the development of competent teachers.

4. That the American Economic Association become an associational affiliate of the National Council for the Social Studies.

5. That a committee be appointed to explore conditions of study and teaching of economics in the schools, and that this committee work as closely as possible with the National Council for the Social Studies and the United States Office of Education. (1950, 623)

The publication of the Taylor Committee's report was approved at the AEA Executive Committee meeting on April 7-8, 1950, but with regard to the other recommendations the minutes read:

The remaining four items of the Committee's recommendations were discussed and the following action taken:

Item 2. -- VOTED to postpone action on establishing a permanent or standing committee on education in economics.

Item 3. -- VOTED to establish an exploratory committee of three on graduate training in economics
with broad terms of reference; namely, the need for
such a study, subjects which should be investigated,
activities and plan of other groups engaged in such
studies, costs and financial sources of assistance
for such a study. . . . Dean Howard R. Bowen has
accepted the chairmanship of this committee and is
to suggest other members for appointment.

Items 4 and 5. -- No action taken. (1951, 767)

The minutes of the December 26 and 30, 1950, Executive
Committee meeting read:

With this (published) report at hand, it was VOTED
to discharge the Committee, with thanks.

A communication from Professor Taylor was read,
asking reconsideration of points 4 and 5 of the committee report of a year ago (see *Papers and Proceedings*, May 1950, 623). A vote was taken to
invite Horace Taylor and Howard R. Bowen to appear before the Committee to answer questions and
explain their recommendations but this vote was re-
scinded. (1951, 767)

These minutes are quoted at some length to give the flavor of
the Executive Committee's reluctance to move beyond the AEA's
traditional position of simply holding roundtable discussions and
publishing papers in the area of economic education, and to also
indicate that the Committee seemed more willing to explore
graduate training in economics than other areas of economics
instruction.

The Bowen Committee on Graduate
Training in Economics

The Executive Committee's final decision to undertake a
study of graduate training in Economics came only after consider-

able debate of a report by a four-person ad hoc committee appointed to study the matter. The committee's report, submitted by Howard R. Bowen, G. L. Bach, Gale Johnson, and I. C. Sharfman, stated:

> In view of our recommendations regarding the selection of the committee and the organization of the study, we believe that the Association should not expect to give formal approval to the study or to the recommendations contained therein. Rather, it should serve as sponsor of the study, it should receive the report and, having satisfied itself that the report is worthy of publication, publish it. Under this plan, the Association would be relieved of the responsibility of achieving broad representation in the membership of the committee; the necessity for effecting compromises among many different views (thus diluting the report) would be avoided; the Association would not be in the position of criticizing, by implication, the graduate program of any university; and the Association would not be put in the position of tacitly attempting to impose standards. In short, our view is that a better and more effective report will be possible if the objective is an imaginative and forceful document rather than a report of which every one approves. On the other hand, we believe that careful selection of the committee, according to the above specifications, will result in a reasoned and responsible report. (951, 792-93)

Following the Executive Committee's approval in April 1951 (1952, 716), a grant was obtained from the Rockefeller Foundation, and Howard R. Bowen was appointed to carry out the study with the assistance of an advisory committee consisting of G. L. Bach, Milton Friedman, I. L. Sharfman, and J. J. Spengler. Bowen's report to the Executive Committee in December 1951 stated:

> The report of the study, when it reaches preliminary form, will be submitted for criticism to the members of the advisory committee and to many other interested persons, and will be revised in light of sug-

gestions offered. However, the contents of the report will be the responsibility of the author rather than of the Association. The latter, as sponsor of the project, will receive the report, and if it is found worthy of publication, publish it. But the Association will not expect to adopt the report as an official declaration on graduate education in economics. (1952, 748)

After completion, the Bowen report, entitled "Graduate Training in Economics," was published as a special supplement to the *AER* in September 1953. This report and its recommendations served as the basis for a roundtable discussion at the 1953 annual meetings, and a six-person "Ad Hoc Committee on Implementation of the Bowen Report" consisting of G. L. Bach, Robert D. Calkins, Robert A. Gordon, John K. Galbraith, Albert G. Hart, and O. J. Brownlee was established in 1954. The minutes of the Executive Committee meetings held on December 28 and 30, 1954, state:

It appeared that little agreement had been reached during preliminary discussions, although all members acknowledged our professional responsibilities with regard to the training of economists and all favored continued study of the recommendations contained in the report. (1955, 651)

And the minutes of the March 25-26, 1955, Executive Committee meeting state:

G. L. Bach elaborated the recommendations made by this committee and explained reasons for points of disagreement among its members. It was VOTED to discharge the committee, with our appreciation. G. L. Bach was requested to discuss certain items with his colleagues and under this narrower scope of reference to report back, possibly at the December meeting. (1956, 586)

But the AEA's Secretary's report for 1955 later stated, "G. L. Bach wrote that he had recanvassed the members of the Ad Hoc

Committee and that none of them felt that the general issues raised last spring need be brought up again." (1956, 594)

The Taylor and Bowen committees were significant because they demonstrated that the AEA could appoint a committee and publish its results without an official endorsement of its conclusions or the need to get complete agreement among its members on the specific contents or recommendations. The Bowen Committee had the added significance of obtaining outside grant funding for its activities. This procedure was later to be used in connection with other economic education activities, particularly the appointment of the National Task Force on Economic Education in 1960. The work of this Task Force, the legacy of which is still with us thirty years later, is by far the most significant set of activities in economics education at the pre-college level ever undertaken by professional economists in this country.

Before turning to the National Task Force on Economic Education, however, it is necessary to trace the evolution of the AEA position on the Taylor Committee's recommendation to establish a standing committee on economic education.

The Ad Hoc Committee on Economics in Teacher Education

In 1952, G. Derwood Baker, Director of the Joint Council on Economic Education, extended an invitation to the AEA Secretary, James Washington Bell, to have the Association cooperate formally with a newly formed Commission on Economics in Teacher Education through an officially appointed AEA Committee on Economics in Teacher Education. In his report for the year Bell stated:

> **I recommend the appointment of such a committee on the grounds that this activity is a legitimate and logical one in which we should participate. Many of our members are interested. If we disregard it, we will have no voice in the determination of policies and activities vitally affecting the profession -- ones which educators themselves are not technically**

qualified to carry on alone. We have made some progress in major fields; e.g., teaching economics on the undergraduate level and graduate training in economics. There still remain the areas of economics in the secondary schools and economics for the layman. The best approach to these areas may well be teaching teachers what to teach and how to teach economics. We should share responsibilities, not only in promoting research, but also promoting education in economics on every level. (1953, 570)

The minutes of the April 3-5, 1952, Executive Committee meeting state:

An invitation from the Council to the AEA to participate in a program of training teachers to teach economics was discussed at length and it was VOTED to authorize the Secretary to accept membership on the Commission on Economics in Teacher Education and in the light of this experience to report on the desirability of further co-operation. (1953, 561)

The minutes of the December 27 and 29, 1952, Executive Committee meeting state:

In conformity with action taken at the April, 1952 meeting, the Secretary accepted membership in the Commission on Economics in Teacher Education and attended an exploratory meeting held in New York City on May 23, 1952. Representatives from the Joint Council on Economic Education and the American Association of Colleges for Teacher Education were present and plans were made for organizing the Commission and formulating its purposes and functions. A second meeting of the Commission was held at Riverdale, New York, August 29-30. Your Secretary was unable to attend but reports were received from G. Derwood Baker, Horace Taylor, B. W. Lewis, and Laurence Leamer. Further progress has since been made and three specific subcommittee projects are under way. In view of these developments and because we see a definite professional responsibility in participating in a promising enterprise which supplements and is complementary to our previous and present endeavors in this field of economic education, it was recommended that the A.E.A. appoint an official Committee on Economics in Teacher Education. It was VOTED to approve this recommendation. The following members have been appointed: B. W. Lewis, Chairman, Horace Taylor, and Archibald McIsaac. (1953, 564)

The Ad Hoc Committee on Economics in Teacher Education made two reports to the Executive Committee in 1953 and 1954, and a roundtable discussion on "Economics in General Education" was held at the annual meetings in 1953. In 1955 the committee presented a third report as the Ad Hoc Committee on Economic Education in which it recommended that its activities and its membership be expanded, and that it be reconstituted as a standing committee on economics education.

The First Standing Committee on Economic Education

The minutes of the December 28 and 30, 1955, Executive Committee meeting state:

It was VOTED to approve the recommendations that this be enlarged and constituted as a standing committee. There was some debate concerning its functions, e.g., whether the Committee was charged with enough or too much work to do, but it is expected that the committee will be able to crystallize ideas concerning this matter, especially after seeing the results of the item on economics in education to be included in the *Directory* questionnaire. (1956, 589)

Clark C. Bloom and Floyd A. Bond were added to Lewis, McIsaac and Strayer to make the new standing committee a five-person committee, and Clark L. Allen was added in 1957 to bring the Committee's membership to six.

A question on member interest in economics education was placed in the 1956 AEA *Directory* questionnaire, and a round-table discussion on "Economics in the Schools" was held at the 1956 annual meeting. The Committee's December 1956, report stated:

> **Thus far, Committee members have taken pains not to identify the Association officially with the Joint Council, but we believe that the time has arrived for a formal affiliation of the Association with the Council to be established. We will bring in a recommendation to this effect at the next meeting of the Executive Committee. . . . A strong movement is clearly under way; it has purpose, form, and energy. Economists are beginning to participate. They should be active in far greater numbers, and they should be nearer to the front.** (1957, 723)

At the Executive Committee meetings on December 27 and 29, 1956, it was voted to accept an invitation of the JCEE to name three representatives of the AEA as members of the Board of Trustees of the Joint Council. Ben W. Lewis, Clark C. Bloom, and Lester V. Chandler were subsequently named to fill these spots.

In 1957 the Joint Council received a grant from the Ford Foundation for the purpose of preparing a cumulative index and register of economists interested in economics education. The AEA Committee co-operated with the JCEE in obtaining this grant and in compiling the register under the direction of Dean Eugene Swearington of Oklahoma State University.

In 1958, the Committee proposed two projects. One was to study "leading textbooks used in secondary school courses in American History, Economics, Social Studies, Problems of Democracy, etc., to learn the nature and coverage of this present economic content." The second was to study "the whole area of social science teaching in secondary schools designed to disclose: (a) what is actually being done (curriculum); (b) the facts regarding the preparation and training of teachers; and (c) the results (testing)." (1959, 605)

The Executive Committee of the AEA authorized the Committee to seek funds to finance these projects, and the Committee's year-end report stated:

> The Committee has been assured, within the last few days, of a grant of $25,000 from the Ford Foundation to enable us to go ahead with our projected study of textbooks used in secondary school courses in American History, Social Studies, and Economics. We have named Paul Olson of Iowa to head the project, and, with the Committee, he is now selecting and engaging reviewers . . . .
>
> Our larger project -- a survey to be undertaken co-operatively with the other social sciences of "The state of the social sciences in the secondary schools" -- is still in the early stages of "negotiation." We are working currently with the Committee on Secondary Schools of the ACLS and shortly we will approach the National Council on Social Studies and the SSRC. (1959, 648)

Following the precedent established by the earlier reports of the Taylor Committee and the Bowen Committee, the AEA Committee's textbook study was eventually published as a special supplement to the March, 1963, *AER* after Professor Olson had given an earlier paper on his committees' preliminary findings at the December 1960 annual meetings (Olson, 1961).

The attempts to work with the ACLS, the NCSS, and SSRC, however, did not make much progress and the Committee's December 1959 report, which was filed by Clark C. Bloom, who served as Acting Chairman while Ben Lewis was abroad, noted:

> The committee has received several requests from state and local educational groups asking a recommendation of economic content for public school courses. No recommendations have been made and these requests have simply been turned over to individual economists who might be interested. (1960, 705-706)

This latter observation called attention to a situation which was apparently discussed in some detail at the AEA's Executive Committee meeting in New York on March 25-26, 1960. The minutes of this meeting state:

> **Special attention was devoted to a proposal from CED that the AEA set up a task force in economic education. After a thorough discussion of the implications of this proposal, it was VOTED to authorize the Committee on Economic Education to explore and to develop a project providing for the creation of a task force on economic education in secondary schools (1) to provide a frame of reference for high school teachers, administrators, and curriculum specialists which clarifies the meaning, nature, content, and methods of economics (at least that portion of economics which should be thought of as the minimum to be understood by all high school graduates) and thus to provide somewhat greater direction for the economic education movement, and (2) to set forth recommendations for a continuing program designed to provide better teaching materials on economics for the public schools. The task force is to be made up of economists of high national reputation. The Committee on Economic Education and the President of the Association are to establish and appoint a group of competent economists and educators to constitute one task force and to receive funds for this purpose from CED and from other sources to carry out the foregoing project.** (1961, 599)

The National Task Force on Economic Education

The AEA's Committee on Economic Education provided the panel of names from which the membership of the National Task Force was chosen by AEA president, T. W. Schultz. G. L. Bach was named Chairman of the Task Force, Floyd A. Bond was named Executive Secretary, and Lester V. Chandler, Robert A.

Gordon, Ben W. Lewis, and Paul A. Samuelson were the other economists appointed to serve along with Arno Bellack and M. L. Frankel, two educators who were appointed as consulting members.

The Task Force began an unprecedented series of activities almost immediately, and the minutes of the Executive Committee meeting held in St. Louis on December 27 and 30, 1960, state:

> **The Task Force recommended that the AEA agree to co-sponsor the Continental Classroom TV program, either in 1961-62 or 1962-63. It was VOTED (by a show of hands, five to one, others not voting) that the AEA co-sponsor the Continental Classroom under the following conditions: (1) that the Executive Committee have a veto over the personnel conducting the program; (2) that the program be postponed to 1962-63; (3) that detailed supervision by the AEA be effected through its members on the National Task Force.** (1961, 602)

The Task Force inevitably assumed some of the former duties of the standing Committee on Economic Education, and the two groups filed separate reports in 1961 and 1962. The cornerstone of the Task Force's work was its report *Economic Education in the Schools*, which was published in September 1961, and served as a topic of discussion at the AEA's annual meetings in December 1962. As indicated previously, "The American Economy" television course, which was broadcast over CBS and PBS stations in 1962-63 and repeated over many public television stations in 1963-64, was an off shoot of the Task Force's work, as were two other activities: one that led to the publication of a report entitled *Study Materials for Economic Education in the Schools* in October, 1961; and the other that led to the publication of a *Test of Economic Understanding* in 1964. Each of these major activities merits a separate paragraph of explanation.

Economic Education in the Schools: Report of the National Task Force on Economic Education was an attempt "to describe the minimum understanding of economics essential for good citizenship and attainable by high school students." It was not a textbook or a lesson plan but more of a checklist of major concepts, issues, institutions, and subject matter aimed at helping students develop the ability to reason about economic problems. Through a grant provided by the Committee for Economic Development, a copy of the Task Force report was sent to every high school in the United States and to a large number of leading educational officials, businessmen, and others interested in economics education. A brief summary of the report was sent to a still wider group, including school board members. The Task Force Chairman estimated "a total of about 150,000 copies was distributed." (1963, 720)

"The American Economy" Television Course consisted of 160 half-hour lessons, thirty-two of which dealt with methods of instruction aimed at teachers who were encouraged to take the course for credit at one of 388 cooperating colleges and universities. Most of the 128 economics content lessons were taught by John R. Coleman of Carnegie Institute of Technology with the advice and assistance of the National Task Force and some forty leading economists and public officials who appeared as guests on individual programs. A full description of the course appeared in the September 1962 *AER* (940-45), and Professor Coleman presented a paper at the 1962 AEA annual meetings (Coleman 1963). The Task Force Chairman estimated a daily viewing audience of between 1,000,000 and 1,250,000 in 1962-63, and noted: "This is far more than have watched any of the preceding nationwide education television programs." (1963, 721)

Study Materials for Economic Education in the Schools was the product of the Joint Council's Materials Evaluation Committee. This committee was chaired by Lewis E. Wagner, and its members were selected with the advice of several major professional associations in addition to the National Task Force. Using the general framework of the task force report, this committee spent the summer of 1961 reviewing some seven thousand pamphlets and other non-textbook teaching materials offered to secondary schools in economics and developed an annotated list of ninety-one supplementary teaching items classified under twenty-one subject headings. The Joint Council subsequently revised and updated this report on several occasions.

The Test of Economic Understanding was developed by a third distinguished professional group under the chairmanship of John Stalnaker, president of the National Merit Scholarship Corporation. Known as the Committee for Measurement of Economic Understanding of the Joint Council on Economic Education, this committee developed two fifty-item sets of multiple-choice questions designed to measure the type of economic understanding outlined in the Task Force Report. The tests and an accompanying *Interpretative Manual and Discussion Guide* were published by Science Research Associates for the Joint Council in 1964. The latest revision of the Test of Economic Understanding is now known as the *Test of Economic Literacy*. (Soper and Walstad 1987, and Walstad and Soper 1988)

Despite the ultimate success and widespread impact of its efforts, the AEA's association with the National Task Force was not unanimously approved. The five-to-one vote of the Executive Committee, with the many abstentions, reported earlier concerning the TV series, gives some indication of the reservations some people may have had, and the minutes of the March 1961 vote to nominate a panel from which the JCEE could appoint an Advisory Committee for its guidance in preparing education materials note "approval of this matter was not unanimous." (1962, 358) George Stigler expressed his personal reservations more directly when he reviewed the Task Force Report at the December 1962 AEA meetings. He noted:

> **Although the American Economic Association explicitly does not endorse the report, it chose the economists and hence certified to their competence and distinction. No other body concerned with economic education has had such professional status, nor is an equally authoritative body likely to appear in this decade. The report will therefore command an audience of unusual size and deference among high school and college teachers.**
>
> **This unusual status is, I believe, unfortunate. The economists composing the Task Force are leaders in American economics, of unquestionable competence and integrity. But they do not monopolize these virtues, and their special mode of selection**

serves to give their views an eminence which is incompatible with the doctrine of free competition (free discussion) in education and scientific work . . . .

The only legitimate complaint -- and I promise not to recur to this point again -- is that some (representative) views have been given a preferential status among non-economists. (1963, 653-54)

Despite the criticism of Stigler and others, the impact of the Task Force report and its associated activities opened new vistas of what might be possible in the way of action-oriented programs in the broad area of economics education. This led to suggestions, later carried out, that the activities of the National Task Force and the AEA's standing Committee on Economic Education be combined in a new, reconstituted AEA Committee on Economic Education.

In 1963 a special Committee on the Future Role of the AEA in Economic Education was appointed with Ben Lewis as Chairman, and G. L. Bach, R. A. Gordon, Abba P. Lerner, W. Allen Wallis, and Harold F. Williamson as members. Williamson was also the Secretary of the AEA at that time. The minutes of the December 26 and 29, 1963, Executive Committee meeting state:

Committee on the Future Role of the AEA in Economic Education (B. W. Lewis). The Chairman presented a written report, published below. Following a discussion, it was VOTED to authorize the President to appoint a new six-man committee to explore the possibilities of improving the quality of economic education at the precollege, college, and adult education levels. Three of the members of this committee are to serve as an advisory committee to the Joint Council on Economic Education. Because of the appointment of this new committee, it was VOTED to dissolve the former Committee on Economic Education. (1964, 641)

The Present Standing Committee on Economic Education

The new six person committee appointed to begin in 1964 consisted of: G. L. Bach, Chairman, R. A. Gordon, Ben W. Lewis, Marshall R. Colberg, Rendigs Fels, and Emanuel T. Weiler. Lewis, Bach, and Fels were named as the members of the JCEE Special Advisory Committee. As part of its mandate, the Committee was commissioned to arrange one session on economics education at each AEA annual meeting, and the proceedings of this session have been published in *The AER Papers and Proceedings* continuously since 1967.

Bach served as chairman of the present committee from 1964 until 1977, when he was succeeded by Allen C. Kelley. Kelley in turn was succeeded as chairman by W. Lee Hansen in 1983, and Hansen was succeeded by John J. Siegfried in 1988. Ben W. Lewis, who served as chairman of the various predecessor committees continuously from 1952 until 1964, continued to serve on the present committee until his retirement in 1967. The committee's 1968 report concluded:

> **The Committee wishes to record a special vote of appreciation to Ben Lewis, who this year ended many years of service on this Committee, for his extraordinary contribution to the cause of better teaching in economics. For over a decade, he has been "Mr. Economic Education" to economists and to educators in the secondary schools. No one has done more to further humane and effective economics teaching. The profession owes him a large debt of gratitude. (1969, 601)**

Under Bach's leadership the committee developed an activist, project-oriented agenda. In addition to advising the JCEE in a variety of areas, the committee was instrumental in:

- Obtaining grants from the National Science Foundation to run a Visiting Scientist Program in Economics from 1967-1972. This program provided for visits of distinguished economists to smaller campuses whose main focus was on undergraduate teaching.

- Obtaining a grant from the Kazanjian Foundation to finance publication of reports on experiments in the teaching of introductory college economics. (Haley 1967a and 1967b)

- Developing a *Test of Understanding College Economics (TUCE)* to parallel the *Test of Economic Understanding* previously developed for use in high schools. (Fels 1967, and Welsh and Fels 1969)

- Stimulating an increased interest in analytical evaluation of economics education activities and in launching a new *Journal of Economic Education* in 1969. The committee served as the first editorial board of this journal, and its first editor was Henry Villard, who was a member of the committee at the time of his appointment.

Not content to rest on these laurels, Bach presented an ambitious "Agenda for Improving the Teaching of Economics" for the committee as a paper at the 1972 annual meetings. In this paper he indicated that a substantial grant had been obtained from the Sloan Foundation to inaugurate a program to train Ph.D. candidates to become better teachers. As it eventually evolved, the *Teacher Training Program (TTP)* resulted in the publication of a *Resource Manual* (Saunders, Welsh, and Hansen, 1978) and a series of national workshops for college and university professors and graduate students were held at Indiana University in 1973 and 1979, the University of Wisconsin in 1980, the University of North Carolina in 1982, and the University of Colorado in 1983. The original Sloan grant was later supplemented by grants from the Lilly Endowment, Exxon Educational Foundation, JM Foundation, City Corporation, Borg Warner, and the JCEE and participating universities. Over three-hundred graduate students and faculty members, representing sixty different colleges and universities, participated in the national TTP programs (Bach and Kelley 1984, 13), and several economics departments throughout the country continue to use TTP materials to train their graduate student instructors.

In 1979 a grant from the Alfred P. Sloan Foundation helped the committee launch a project to study the undergraduate economics major under the direction of John J. Siegfried. Siegfried's work resulted in a major presentation at the December 1981 AEA meetings. (Siegfried and Wilkinson 1982)

As the result of the committee's emphasis on hard research at many of the sessions on economics education at the AEA annual meetings and the development of *The Journal of Economic Education*, Siegfried and Fels could report:

A cumulative literature on economics education has now developed. . . . The quality of the research done so far varies widely, but dramatic improvement has occurred in recent years; much more of the current research is first rate than was the case 15 years ago. . . . The field is rapidly becoming respectable, and the research findings can be useful to college economics teaching. (1979, 959)

The committee later cooperated with the JCEE in obtaining a grant from the Pew Trust to fund a project aimed at attracting more younger economists into research on economics education. Seminars were held at Princeton University in the summers of 1987 and 1988, and participants presented some of their work at JCEE organized sessions at the AEA annual meetings in December 1988 and 1989.

The Test of Understanding in College Economics was revised in 1980 (Saunders, Fels, and Welsh 1981) and is currently being revised again. Beginning in 1985 the committee began working with the Joint Council on plans for an advanced placement program in economics that was implemented during the 1988-89 academic year. (Buckles and Morton 1988) The committee co-sponsored a conference on the state of economics principles textbooks with the *Journal of Economic Education* in September 1987, and it has cooperated with the independent Commission on Graduate Economic Education in Economics, which sponsored a session at the December 1989 AEA meetings. The committee is also continuing its research on the economics major in cooperation with the Association of American Colleges.

It is clear from this list of activities that the AEA Committee on Economic Education has come a long way since the initial reluctance of the Association's Executive Committee to appoint a standing committee in this area. The current committee sees itself as having the following six broad responsibilities:

1. Enhancing recognition within the profession of the impor-
    tance of effective teaching.

2. Facilitating the training of more effective economics teachers.

3. Improving the assessment of what and how much our stu-
    dents learn.

4. Cooperating with and assisting the JCEE (with its primary
    mission of improving precollege economics education).

5. Encouraging innovation in teaching methods and research on
    teaching effectiveness.

6. Disseminating information about effective economics teach-
    ing. (1990, 484)

Having now traced in some detail the steps that have been taken in getting an increasing number of economists involved in economics education, this article will conclude with a consider-ation of the rationales or arguments that have been used to justify this activity.

Justifying Rationales

In arguing that it should be made a standing committee, the Ad Hoc Lewis Committee stated:

**It probably does not need to be argued here that
over the years the preservation and effective operation of our economic and governmental system will
depend upon an alert and informed people. Increasingly, the problems that confront our people
both as participants in our political economy and as**

voters are economic in character. Increasingly in modern society, economic understanding is required of each of us as a condition for personal satisfaction and development and for our common economic and political well-being. To teach economic understanding to the great bulk of our population is the task, first, of the schools; but it is the responsibility of professional economists on the staffs of our colleges and universities to teach the teachers of economics in the schools and to give continuing guidance and support to their teaching efforts. . . .

The economics profession will greatly misjudge its responsibility in our society if it continues its long-time indifference to the place and problems of economics in the schools and evidences professional concern for economics only at the college and graduate levels. Serious professional work in this area by economists needs to be given professional support and it needs to be accorded professional status. It needs professional recognition by this Association. Specifically, this Association should establish a standing Committee on Economic Education. (1956, 619-621)

Later, in a paper presented at the annual meetings of the AEA in 1956, Lewis stated:

It took about fifteen minutes to convince the Executive committee that the economics profession has a deep and positive responsibility in this area. It remains to be seen how long it will take for the individual members of the economics profession to become aware of this responsibility, to define its shape and content, to accept the responsibility and to give positive, purposeful expression to their acceptance. . . .

I have heard it said that economists with an eye to their professional future cannot afford to devote themselves to the problems of economics in the schools. Work at this level is professionally not quite respectable. It lacks professional status. I suspect it is true that most of our work at this level does not carry professional status, but I also suspect that in contemplating this situation we are inclined to confuse cause and effect. Certainly nothing that economists undertake is prompted by a purpose worthier than the improvement of economic education in the schools and the development of economic understanding among all of our people; and certainly nothing that economists undertake is more professionally challenging, if we measure challenges by the difficulties which must be faced by those who accept them. May I suggest, then, that professional status in this area is present, but latent: it awaits professional performance. Status will be abundantly present and evident for any of us who bring to this task a quality of professional performance worthy of professional status. (Lewis, 1956, 654 and 667)

In a paper presented four years later, G. L. Bach used the following, somewhat similar, arguments:

The basic case for economics in the high schools is the case for democracy itself. Democracy means government by the people. Government affairs, in very substantial part, are economic affairs. High school students of today, as the citizens of tomorrow, will work and live as part of an economic system, which they must understand at least reasonably well to function as effective citizens. For democracy to work on economic issues, the people must understand; it is not enough that the leaders alone do so.

Given the fact that only 10 or 15 percent of today's high school students will probably take a course in economics in college, it is simply irresponsible for economists to say we should not bother to teach economics in the high schools. The real alternative is for the vast majority of citizens to study no economics at all. We merely kid ourselves when we assume that the college economics course

59

is the solution to the problem for the foreseeable future.

Only if a little teaching of economics in the high schools must be worse than none at all can the prevailing attitude of the profession be justified. The fact that economics, in separate courses or more generally in history or problems in democracy courses, is in fact so badly taught that it may be worse than nothing at all, is no justification for our refusing to touch the high school problem. On the contrary, it makes more evident the need for professional economists to help in improving the quality of the economics that is taught in the schools. (1961, 581)

The most recent CEE report puts a somewhat more modern twist to its rationale when it states:

Committee members argued that the demand for publicly provided services like those produced by the committee should be grounded in some private market failure. The Committee has historically emphasized the creation and dissemination of information about effective teaching methods. This fits the market failure criterion, as information is frequently subject to scale economies, free-rider and externality problems, and is available to additional users at close to zero marginal cost. (1990, 484)

Whether for the reasons presented here, or for others, there is little doubt that the AEA's standing Committee on Economic Education now has an acceptance and a set of activities that could have been little dreamed of when the Taylor Committee first recommended that such a committee be created in 1949.

References

Bach, G. L. 1961. "Economics in the High Schools: The Responsibility of the Profession." *American Economic Review,
Papers and Proceedings*, 51:2, 579-586.

_____. 1973. "An Agenda for Improving the Teaching
of Economics." *American Economic Review, Papers and
Proceedings*. 63:2, 303-308.

_____, and Allen C. Kelley. 1984. "Improving the
Teaching of Economics: Achievements and Aspirations."
American Economic Review, Papers and Proceedings.
74:2, 12-18.

Bowen, Howard R. 1953. "Graduate Education in Economics."
American Economic Review. 43:4, Part 2, i-223.

Buckles, Stephen, and John S. Morton. 1988. "The Effects of
Advanced Placement on College Introductory Economics
Courses," *American Economic Review, Papers and
Proceedings*. 78:2, 263-268.

Coats, A. W. 1985. "The American Economic Association and the
Economics Profession." *Journal of Economic Literature*.
23:4, 1697-1727.

Coleman, John R. 1963. "Economic Literacy: What Role for
Television." *American Economic Review, Papers and
Proceedings*. 53:2, 645-52.

"College of the Air's 'The American Economy.'" 1962. *American
Economic Review*. 52:4, 940-45.

"Economics in the Schools: A Report by a Special Textbook
Study Committee of the Committee on Economic Education
of the American Economic Association." 1963. *American
Economic Review*. 53:1, Part 2, i-27.

Economic Education in the Schools: Report of the National Task Force on Economic Education. 1961. New York: Committee for Economic Development.

Fels, Rendigs. 1967. "A New 'Test of Understanding in College Economics.'" *American Economic Review, Papers and Proceedings.* 57:2, 660-666.

Haley, Bernard F. 1967a. "Experiments in the Teaching of Basic Economics." *American Economic Review, Papers and Proceedings.* 57:2, 642-561.

_____. 1967b. *Experiments in the Teaching of Basic Economics.* New York: Joint Council on Economic Education.

Hewett, William H. 1951. "Divergent Views of Members of the Subcommittee on Teaching the Elementary Course in Economics." *American Economic Review.* 41:3, 428-431.

Leamer, Laurence E. 1950a. "A Brief History of Economics in General Education." *American Economic Review.* 40:5, Part 2, 18-33.

_____. 1950b. "A Selected Bibliography on Economics in General Education." Ibid, 202-213.

Lewis, Ben W. 1957. "Economic Understanding: Why and What." *American Economic Review, Papers and Proceedings.* 47:2, 653-670.

Olson, Paul R. 1961. "This is Economics in the Schools." *American Economic Review, Papers and Proceedings.* 51:2, 564-70.

Saunders, Phillip, Arthur L. Welsh, and W. Lee Hansen, Eds. 1978. *Resource Manual for Teacher Training Programs in Economics.* New York: Joint Council on Economic Education.

_____, Rendigs Fels, and Arthur L. Welsh. 1981. "The Revised Test of Understanding College Economics." *American Economic Review, Papers and Proceedings*. 71:2, 190-194.

Siegfried, John J. and Rendigs Fels. 1979. "Research on Teaching College Economics: A Survey." *Journal of Economic Literature*. 17:3, 923-969.

_____, and James T. Wilkinson. 1982. "The Economics Curriculum in the United States: 1980." *American Economic Review, Papers and Proceedings*. 72:2, 125-138.

Soper, John C. and William B. Walstad. 1987. *The Test of Economic Literacy (2nd Ed.): Examiner's Manual*. New York: Joint Council on Economic Education.

Stigler, George J. 1963. "Elementary Economic Education." *American Economic Review, Papers and Proceedings*. 53:2, 653-659.

Study Materials for Economic Education in the Schools: Report of the Materials Evaluation Committee. 1961. New York: Joint Council on Economic Education.

Test of Economic Understanding: Interpretive Manual and Discussion Guide. 1964. Chicago: Science Research Associates.

Walstad, William B. and John C. Soper. 1988. "A Report Card on the Economic Literacy of U.S. High School Students." *American Economic Review, Papers and Proceedings*. 78:2, 251-256.

Welsh, Arthur L. and Rendigs Fels. 1969. "Performance on the New Test of Understanding College Economics." *American Economic Review, Papers and Proceedings*. 59:2, 224-229.

APPENDIX I

48	1958	No report
49	1959	Report of the Committee on Economic Education, Ben W. Lewis, 648.
50	1960	Report of the Committee on Economic Education, Clark C. Bloom, 705-06.
51	1961	Report of the Committee on Economic Education, Ben W. Lewis, 638.
52	1962	Report of the Committee on Economic Education, Ben W. Lewis, 575.
		National Task Force on Economic Education, G. L. Bach, 576.
53	1963	Committee on Economic Education, Ben W. Lewis, 719.
		Report of the National Task Force on Economic Education, G. L. Bach, 720.
		Report of the Special Publications Advisory Committee to Joint Council on Economic Education, G. L. Bach, 723.
54	1964	Report of the Committee on the Future Role of the AEA in Economic Education, Ben W. Lewis, 672.
55	1965	Report of the Committee on Economic Education, G. L. Bach, Marshall Colberg, Rendigs Fels, R. A. Gordon, Ben W. Lewis, E. T. Weiler, 615-18.
56	1966	Report of the Committee on Economic Education, G. L. Bach, 637-39.
57	1967	Report of Committee on Economic Education, G. L. Bach, 709-10.

58	1968	Report of Committee on Economic Education, G. L. Bach, 723-24.
59	1969	Report of Committee on Economic Education, G. L. Bach, 600-01.
60	1970	Report of Committee on Economic Education, G. L. Bach, 515-16.
61	1971	Report of Committee on Economic Education, G. L. Bach, 505-06.
62	1972	No Report
63	1973	No report, but a paper "An Agenda for Improving the Teaching of Economics" by G. L. Bach was published in the Papers part of the *Papers and Proceedings*, 303-08
64	1974	Report of Committee on Economic Education, G. L. Bach, 512-13.
65	1975	Report of Committee on Economic Education, G. L. Bach, 506-07.
66	1976	Report of Committee on Economic Education, G. L. Bach, 523-24.
67	1977	No Report
68	1978	No Report
69	1979	Report of the Committee on Economic Education, W. Lee Hansen, 426-27.
70	1980	Report of the Committee on Economic Education, Allen C. Kelley, 478.
71	1981	Report of the Committee on Economic Education, Allen C. Kelley, 481.
72	1982	No Report

73	1983	Report of the Committee on Economic Education, Allen C. Kelley, 412.
74	1984	No report, but a paper "Improving the Teaching of Economics: Achievements and Aspirations," by G. L. Bach and Allen C. Kelley was published in the Papers part of the *Papers and Proceedings*, 12-18.
75	1985	Report of the Committee on Economic Education, W. Lee Hansen, 455.
76	1986	Report of the Committee on Economic Education, W. Lee Hansen, 458.
77	1987	Report of the Committee on Economic Education, W. Lee Hansen, 392-93.
78	1988	Report of the Committee on Economic Education, W. Lee Hansen, 518-19.
79	1989	Report of the Committee on Economic Education, John Siegfried, 420-21.
80	1990	Report of the Committee on Economic Education, John J. Siegfried, 483-84.

APPENDIX II

PAPERS AND DISCUSSIONS ON ECONOMIC EDUCATION
TOPICS PUBLISHED IN THE PAPERS SECTION OF
*THE AMERICAN ECONOMIC REVIEW, PAPERS AND
PROCEEDINGS* SINCE 1950

Vol 54, No. 2, May 1964
Efficiency in the Teaching of Economics: The Product

Vol 55, No. 2, May 1965
Economic Education: Experiments in the Teaching of Economics

Vol 57, No. 2 May 1967
The Efficiency of Education in Economics

70

U.S. GOVERNMENT POLICY, STATE EDUCATION MANDATES, AND ECONOMICS EDUCATION

Stephen Buckles

This discussion explains the case for economics education by examining relevant federal law and agencies for references to the importance of economics education to major economic policy debate and issues and by considering the major state legislation affecting the delivery of economics education. These efforts resulted in a conclusion that federal legislation itself has not considered economics education. However, several agencies and individuals within those agencies have taken active economics education roles. State law has been much more active. The majority of our students are in states that require a significant role for economics education within the curriculum.

The Joint Economic Committee

The Employment Act of 1946 has the stated purpose "of creating and maintaining, in a manner calculated to foster and promote free competitive enterprise, the general welfare . . . and employment opportunities and to promote maximum employment, production, and purchasing power." The Act created the Joint Economic Committee to examine current economic conditions and to make appropriate policy recommendations. That committee played a unique role until 1974 when the Congressional Budget Office and Budget Committees in the U.S. House and Senate were created. These Congressional committees have largely supplanted the role of the Joint Economic Committee. Although the Joint Economic Committee has been described as the world's largest economics class, nowhere in the Employment Act of 1946 is an economics education role prescribed or defined for that committee or for the federal government.

Reports of the Joint Economic Committee received wide attention and were normally reviewed and described in the *New York Times*, the *Washington Post*, the *Wall Street Journal*, and other national newspapers. Reports from hearings of the House and Senate Budget Committees and reports from the Congressional Budget Office and the Council of Economic Advisers have been primarily examined by professionals and Congressional staff members. In this manner, those committees and offices have fulfilled an economics education role only indirectly.

The Council of Economic Advisers

The purpose of the President's Council of Economic Advisers is "to provide economic analysis and advice to the President and thus to assist in the development and implementation of national economic policy." While there is no legal indication of a public economics education role, chairmen of the Council have often taken very active roles as economics educators, often with considerable controversy. Others have viewed their roles as very definitely restricted to internal communication.

The first Council chairman, Edwin Nourse, believed that his proper role was limited to providing advice to the president and his cabinet. However, Nourse was active in the founding of the Joint Council on Economic Education and for a time served as its vice chairman. He was followed by Leon Keyserling, who believed that he should be outspoken in educating the public and in advocating the administration's policies. Keyserling was followed by Arthur Burns and Raymond Saulnier, both of whom believed their roles should be restricted to providing advice to the president and the president's cabinet. Burns, however, fulfilled the role of an advocate, somewhat more than Saulnier, and eventually more than Keyserling. Some observers believe that the Council of Economic Advisers under Burns made the public much more sensitive to economic policies and problems.

Walter Heller's term of office saw an increasing role for education and advocacy. President John F. Kennedy instructed him "to use the White House as a pulpit for economics education." Walter Heller took the role seriously and attempted to educate the public before policy decisions were publicly proposed. Kennedy's policy was that we should educate and then make a policy move. Lyndon Johnson's policy was the opposite: we should move first, and the move -- in and of itself -- would provide economics education to the public. Gardner Ackley and Arthur Okun did participate in making speeches and holding press conferences, but not nearly to the extent that Walter Heller did. President Richard Nixon believed that his cabinet members should speak out on economic policy, but gave specific instructions to the Council of Economic Advisers that they should only speak to small groups of professionals. Still, Herbert Stein believed that his proper role was a national one and that he should be providing economics education.

The variance in the opinions of Council chairmen continues to date, with one extreme being represented by Alan Greenspan. He believed that the Council of Economic Advisers should be a research, consultative group for the President. In fact, he even canceled the Council's regular monthly press conferences. On the other extreme was Martin Feldstein, who viewed his role as one of education and even went so far as, in effect, to criticize some of the administration's economic policies. The current chairman, Michael Boskin, has stated that he believes economics education is one of his primary roles.

State Economics Education Mandates

An increasing number of state governments are passing legislation mandating economics education in one form or another. According to the latest available data, twenty-eight states require some type of economics education. Those states are Alabama, Arizona, California, Connecticut, Delaware, Florida, Georgia, Hawaii, Idaho, Illinois, Indiana, Louisiana, Maryland, Nevada, New Hampshire, New York, North Carolina, Oregon, Pennsylvania, Rhode Island, South Carolina, South Dakota, Tennessee, Texas, Utah, Virginia, West Virginia, and Wyoming. The twenty-eight states include two-thirds of the nation's students. Three other states include substantive economics within statewide testing. An additional three states have state departments of education that include economics concepts among their recommended basic standards for the state curriculum. In essence, thirty-four state governments encourage economics education.

The content of these mandates varies considerably. Some mandates require examination of the free enterprise system. One goes so far as to require instruction in the "benefits of the free enterprise system." Others include consumer education. Most, particularly those passed in recent years, mandate what many people would recognize as the teaching of basic economics concepts.

Twelve states require infusion of economics education throughout the kindergarten-to-twelfth-grade curriculum. Seven states require a separate course for graduation while nine states require infusion and a separate course for graduation, for a total of sixteen states. (One of those actually requires only college-bound students to take a separate course.) Four additional states require schools to offer a separate course; fifty percent of the nation's students must take an economics course to graduate.

While state mandates are becoming more common, there is strong resistance in some states. Mandates requiring infusion of economics have been repealed in Mississippi and Oklahoma. Consumer education mandates in Kentucky and Wisconsin have also been repealed.

REFERENCES

Flash, Edward S., Jr. 1965. *Economic Advice and Presidential Leadership: The Council of Economic Advisers.* New York: Columbia University.

Hargrove, Irwin C. and Samuel A Morley. 1984. *The President and the Council of Economic Advisers.* Boulder, Colorado: Westview Press.

Highsmith, Robert J. 1989. *A Survey of State Mandates for Economics Instruction.* New York: Joint Council on Economic Education.

Norton, Hugh S. 1977. *Employment Act in the Council of Economic Advisers, 1946-1976.* Columbia, South Carolina: University of South Carolina Press.

Pfiffner, James P. 1986. *The President and Economic Policy.* Philadelphia: The Institute for the Study of Human Issues.

Schick, Allan. 1983. *Making Economic Policy in Congress.* Washington, D.C.: The American Enterprise Institute.

GOALS, RATIONALE, AND STRATEGIES EMPLOYED BY ECONOMICS EDUCATION ORGANIZATIONS: A SUMMARY AND ANALYSIS

Calvin A. Kent
and
Dennis Weidenaar

In attempting to answer the question, "Why is economics education important, perhaps even essential?" the Society of Economic Educators decided to survey the leading organizations in the United States and Canada who actively support or conduct economics education programs. Sixty-six organizations listed in the *Directory of Organizations Providing Business and Economic Education Information*, were contacted and asked to supply the goals, rationale, and implementation strategies that undergirded their organization's program. Specifically, the organizations were asked to supply copies of their mission statements including the goals and objectives of the organization plus a statement of how they went about implementing these goals and objectives through their programs. Of those organizations queried, twenty-six provided information.

What follows is a compilation of the responses received, divided into three parts. Part I provides a synthesis reflecting the various organizations' goals and reasons for their activities (rationale). Part II outlines the strategies employed by the respondents to achieve the goals. Part III is a summary for each respondent of its goals, rationales, and strategies.

Part I
Goals and Rationales

By way of summary, it is fair to say that a number of the responding organizations assume that the case for economics education either has been made or is so obvious that it does not need to be explicitly stated. Few of the organizations in any way seek to establish a specific need or rationale for economics education. The general supposition is that economics education is good and the more of it the better.

The goals for most of the organizations included in this analysis fall under five general categories:

1. **Provide understandings that are essential for success in the marketplace.** This is the goal of *practicality*. It stresses that students and others need to understand how the market operates if they are to succeed in it. Failure to grasp this fundamental knowledge will lead to inappropriate decisions that, in turn, will lead to a less rewarding and less productive life. The practicality goal sees economics education as an essential survival skill of great personal benefit to its possessor.

2. **Create a better awareness and understanding of the American economy and the free enterprise system.** This is the most frequently cited goal in the material furnished to the authors by the organizations. This can be called the *awareness* goal. The corollary to this goal says that if the American economic system is better understood, it will be more enthusiastically supported, and its perpetuation -- along with its inherent benefits -- will continue. The awareness goal assumes that the market economy, property rights, economic freedom, and entrepreneurship are self-evident virtues.

3. **Provide an understanding of economic issues so voters can make more intelligent decisions.** This *citizenship* goal is closely tied to the previous one, but here awareness is translated into action. Advocacy often is seen as an adjunct to information. Faced with the myriad economic issues that public policy decision makers must face at all levels of government, those who defend the citizenship goal see an understanding of economics as the only means of ensuring rational political decision making. The assumption is that an economically literate population will elect economically rational policy makers.

4. **Demonstrate the relationship between economic and political liberty.** This *philosophical* goal presumes that there is an inseparable link between economic freedom and other freedoms. If economic freedom is destroyed or reduced, the result will be the dissipation of other freedoms. Economic freedom is seen as an essential part of the free society. This goal sees a universal yearning of people to be free and without economic freedom, that yearning goes unfulfilled.

5. **Show that economic freedom is an essential part of a moral and just society.** This *morality* rationale sees an understanding of economics as a requirement of both material and moral improvement. While encompassing and borrowing from the other goals, it asks deeper philosophical questions. Economics education is justified because it is necessary to understand how free markets work. Why is it necessary to understand how free markets work? Because free markets with property rights and voluntary exchange create economic efficiency. Why is economic efficiency good? Economic efficiency means that resources are used in the most productive manner. Individuals are not coerced into making exchanges that do not better themselves. Economic growth is promoted, thereby enlarging the possibility of expanded material well-being. While material well-being, the happiness of consumers, and the efficiency of producers may be sufficient goals within themselves, these goals presumably promote the good of all people by creating the environment in which economic justice cannot only be debated but also created.

6. **Enhance the capacity for rational decision making.** While rarely explicitly stated in the policy statements furnished, the goal of *rationality* is sometimes implied. It says that individuals need to learn how to make decisions, and at the basis of decision making, is the concept of "trade-offs." One thing must be given up in order to gain another. The skills acquired by learning economic analysis not only provide for rational economic decisions, but also provide a framework and approach for rational decision making in all aspects of an individual's life. Economics education provides a set of

insights and skills that are highly transferrable to all phases of a person's life.

Traditionally, the rationale for economics education has been that all individuals are producers, consumers, and voters. As such, they need to have an understanding of economics if they are to make intelligent decisions in the marketplace and the polling booth. For most of the organizations surveyed, this rationale is sufficient.

Part II
Strategies

The information supplied by the various organizations indicates that several strategies are employed. For lack of a better taxonomy, these strategies can be lumped under two headings, basic and applied. The basic strategy consists of:

- Sponsoring research.

- Conducting workshops and symposiums designed to stimulate thought among scholars and the general public.

- Publication of books, journals, and articles reflecting the organization's views.

The applied strategy stresses:

- Teacher training.

- Production of materials for classroom use.

- Publication of research studies in a format that will sway public opinion to a course of action.

The organizations we surveyed neatly divide themselves within these two categories. Several are concerned with the broader philosophical issues of liberty, economic justice, and personal freedom. Free market economics is seen as a force underlying and essential to those virtues. Encouraging philosophical discourse and discovery and the dissemination of these discoveries, are the prime strategies employed by organizations that take this approach. Few of these organizations focus either on students or teachers.

By far the largest group of organizations, takes the practical or applied route. Many of these organizations provide either materials or training that encompasses the entire educational spectrum from kindergarten through high school. Others focus on specific grades or specific subject areas such as business, marketing, vocational education, or early adolescence.

Some of the organizations provide textbooks and other materials to be used by students in the classroom. Many have produced videos, games, and simulations. Others seek to expand the interface between the classroom and the business community either by bringing business leaders to the classrooms as resource people or by having students, through field trips or other experiences, gain a feel for the process of free enterprise. Many of these groups produce materials for teacher workshops which focus on specific economics issues. Some take an integrating approach, seeing economics as a thread that should be woven into the total fabric of a student's education at as many grade levels and as many subject areas as possible. Others tend to emphasize separate programs with an intense focus upon economics principles and practices.

What is surprising is that, at least in their public statements, few of these organizations tie their strategies back to their rationales and goals. They assume that what they do is needed and that what they are doing is successful in meeting those needs. Perhaps the failure of most organizations to more clearly define their goals and state their rationale, can then be explained. To do so would lead to increased accountability, for it could then be determined whether the strategies they employ actually produce the results they have promised.

Part III
Summary Statements By Organization

Americans for the Competitive Enterprise Systems (ACES), Delaware

ACES represents more than 475 businesses in Delaware, Maryland, and Pennsylvania. It is the belief of these businesses that American life represents one of the best hopes and dreams of humankind, that free enterprise is essential to the quality of American life, and competitive enterprise is the most efficient way to provide society with quality goods and services, economic justice, and personal opportunity.

ACES believes that public understanding of the economy affects the success of its own firms as well as the future of the competitive enterprise system. That is why it dedicates its programs to "inspiring excellence in economics education." It promotes American business and explores economics issues. From its own first-hand business experience, it seeks to correct what it feels are misconceptions while articulating economics concepts. It seeks to help teachers and students appreciate more fully the benefits and challenges of a competitive enterprise system.

It works with teachers by conducting seminars in schools and at business sites. In addition, it distributes materials around which entire courses can be structured, circulates films and filmstrips, develops materials for in-service training of educators, provides speakers on business topics, sponsors luncheon meetings for teachers, and presents nationally prominent speakers on economics to various groups.

The American Enterprise Institute for Public Policy Research (AEI), Washington, D.C.

The purpose of the AEI is to study and understand the issues facing our country, to be engaged in the policy debate without being preoccupied with the headlines of the moment, to offer blunt criticism without losing sight of the great virtues of our political and economic system. These services are not in urgent day-to-day demand in Washington -- yet, Washington cannot survive without them.

AEI feels the nation lives in a time when everyone is infatuated with the short-run. Government officials say this about business executives, business executives say it about politicians, the older generation says it about the younger generations, almost everyone says it about Keynes. AEI's specialty is to advance a long-run view in a short-run city in defense, foreign, economic, and social policy, as well as in the preservation of our political institutions. AEI works by sponsoring seminars and by an extensive publication program of high quality.

The American Institute for Economic Research (AIER), Great Barrington, Massachusetts

The American Institute for Economic Research was founded as an independent scientific and educational organization. The Institute's research is planned to help individuals protect their personal interests and those of the nation. By publishing the results of scientific inquiry carried on with "diligence, independence, and integrity," the AIER hopes to help citizens preserve the best of the nation's future. The Institute represents no fund, concentration of wealth, or other special interests.

The AIER states that experience suggests that information and advice on economic subjects are more useful when they come from a source that is independent of special interests, either commercial or political. The purposes of the Institute are to conduct scientific research in the general economics field and to disseminate the results of such research in order to educate individual students and the general public, so that there may be more widespread understanding of the fundamental economic relationships affecting the citizens of the United States, both as individuals and as members of a complex society. The ultimate objective of this is advancing the welfare of the American people.

As scientists, economists have the humble task of ascertaining and describing economic relationships. However, economic events do not occur in isolation from other social events. On the contrary, economic relationships are an integral aspect of social relationships, and the boundaries of strict economic events within all social transactions frequently are not clear. The AIER strives to clarify those issues.

Association for Private Enterprise Education (APEE), Martin, Tennessee

APEE was established to create a network for holders of academic chairs in private enterprise and entrepreneurship along with directors of economics education and entrepreneurship organizations. APEE is unashamed of its belief in the market system and the entrepreneurial spirit which propels it. APEE believes that private property, voluntary exchange, limited govern-ment, and competitive markets are essential for economic free-dom and that economic freedom is essential if any form of liberty is to endure.

APEE publishes a newsletter and an academic journal. Each year it holds an annual international convention. It sponsors or co-sponsors programs and publications. It also serves as a clearinghouse for both people and projects which share its philos-ophy. Consulting services are provided to universities and colleg-es wishing to start chairs or other programs. APEE sees itself as a clearinghouse for other organizations.

Committee for Economic Development (CED), New York, New York

CED is not so much involved in economics education as it is a "problem detective and consensus builder." CED tries to identify the major long-term economic problems threatening our society and propose sound and workable solutions to deal with them. Their by-laws state:

> **It should be the responsibility of the research and policy committees to develop, through objective research and informed discussion, findings and recommendations for private and public policy that will contribute to preserving and strengthening our**

free society, achieving steady economic growth at high employment and reasonably stable prices, increasing productivity and living standards, providing greater and more equal opportunity for every citizen, and improving the quality of life for all.

The CED is a leading proponent of economics education in grades 7 through 10. It has pioneered the use of innovative case studies to teach young adolescents how America's economic system works. Using the teaching method advocated by the CED, materials have been developed that bring economics concepts and ideas to life through descriptions of how everyday products are made and used. By minimizing the abstractions and technical vocabulary, the CED's new approach to economics education captures student interest while providing them with concrete economic knowledge, practical decision-making skills, and more positive attitudes towards the economy.

Center on Education and Training for Employment (CETE), Ohio State University, Columbus, Ohio

The Center is part of the School of Education for Ohio State University and has as its mission facilitating the career and occupational preparation and advancement of youth and adults. The Center fulfills this mission by conducting applied research, evaluation, and policy analysis. It also provides leadership development, technical assistance, and curriculum development and information services to teachers, school districts, education organizations, state agencies, and officials.

The Center is involved in the promotion of economics education through its national entrepreneurship education consortium consisting of twenty-seven states and nine universities. Their primary strategy for enhancing economics understanding is through curriculum intervention, which takes the form of infusion of entrepreneurship education into existing programs and courses. For twenty-three years the Center has been a national leader in research and development of programs primarily focused on vocational education students.

The Center for the Study of American Business (CSAB), Washington, University, St. Louis, Missouri

The Center was established to enhance public understanding of the private enterprise system and to foster an environment in which private enterprise can prosper. Its scholarly research findings are disseminated to a wide audience of opinion leaders in business, government, academia, and the media throughout the United States. The activities of the Center cover the spectrum of academic and public policy research affecting the private enterprise system. Their programs range from fundamental academic research at one end of the spectrum to a policy-oriented publications program aimed at broad education of the general public at the other.

The Center for Strategic and International Studies (CSIS), Georgetown University, Washington, D.C.

The Georgetown University Center has broader goals than just economics education. The stated purpose of CSIS is to challenge the way people -- especially policymakers -- understand the world. The Center's founders were concerned that the United State's foreign policy was depending too much on purely military and economic power. The CSIS emphasized balanced, interdisciplinary, and anticipatory approaches to a range of foreign and defense policy issues.

The Center's purpose is not advocacy; its leadership believes that progress on compelling issues is served by solid analysis and insight rather than prescriptions. The CSIS does not take specific policy positions.

Distributive Education Clubs of America (DECA), Reston, Virginia

DECA has, as its focus, marketing education. DECA is not an extracurricular activity but is an integrated part of the marketing education program in the high schools throughout the nation. DECA sees itself as a vital link between the classroom and the business world, as a bridge between school and productive employment. All of DECA's activities are based upon an essential truth that there is no personal or political freedom without a free economy. As such, all DECA activities involve the teaching of economics and free enterprise as is stated in the DECA creed:

I believe in the democratic philosophies of private enterprise and competition and in the freedom of this nation -- that these philosophies allow for the fullest development of my individual abilities.

DECA's principle delivery mechanism is through a series of competitions in over seventeen areas related to marketing education. These competitions are organized at the local, state, and national level. Top-ranked winners receive trophies, cash, and awards of corporate stock. It is DECA's goal to produce the next generation of business leaders who possess the skills needed by business as well as an in-depth understanding of the operations and benefits of the free enterprise economy.

The Economic Education Resource Center (EERC), Vancouver, British Columbia

The EERC has as its basic role the encouragement of a better understanding of the principles of economics and their practical application. The Center's prime concern is the improvement of economics and business education at the high school level. Its principle function is to make a comprehensive collection of existing economics education resource materials readily accessible to school teachers, librarians, and counselors. In addition to making existing resources available, the Center encourages the creation and development of new learning materials where a need emerges. The EERC was established in recognition of the fact that economics education is becoming increasingly important with a growing role to play in the curriculum.

Economic Institute for Research and Education (EIRE), Boulder, Colorado

EIRE was created to research and advance the American free enterprise system, and to provide ideas that will serve as the basis for understanding the role of free enterprise in American society.

The Institute's founders believe that the only moral, practical, and workable society is one based on the voluntary exchange process of the free market unhampered by needless government intervention. Ideas are the key to understanding the free enterprise system which was established in this nation by the founding fathers. But in the opinion of EIRE, those ideas are fast eroding. Only through development and dissemination of a philosophy of free enterprise can these frightening trends be reversed and basic liberties of American society be preserved. EIRE believes that through research and communication the ideas of liberty and free enterprise can again become meaningful.

This Institute is a center for professional economists who focus their efforts on research, publication, seminars, and educational programs to promote understanding of the realities of economic survival for businesses, labor, government, and the general public.

Future Business Leaders of America (FBLA), Washington, D.C.

Future Business Leaders of America fully supports the teaching of economics at the secondary and post-secondary levels because the knowledge of economics principles is important to anyone entering the business world today.

FBLA sees economics education as an integral part of business education. Members of FBLA are afforded the opportunity to be in contact with community business leaders where they learn economics principles from a real-life perspective. Members participate in competitive events focused on economics and entrepreneurship in addition to other business skills.

The Foundation for Economic Education (FEE), Irvington-on-the-Hudson, New York

The Foundation is a first-source in supporting individuals concerned about liberty. The Foundation works to improve the individuals understanding of the free market, private property, limited government, and its philosophical antecedents. To this end, FEE has remained a consistent proponent of the ideal concept of human liberty and a critic of collectivism in its many forms. FEE's assignment is for the staff, and the growing number of people who voluntarily associate with it, to develop a better understanding of this philosophy while exploring ways of explaining it with ever improving clarity.

The method used explains how the free market makes for social harmony and peace. The Foundation does not participate in the political process; instead, it presents the rationale of limited government. It takes no sides on specific legislation; instead, it sets forth the broad principles that should underlie the law.

FEE publishes a forty-page monthly study journal. It also conducts a number of summer seminars, regional seminars, on-campus activities, seminars for undergraduates, and essay contests, in addition to activities with high school students.

The Free Enterprise Institute (FEI), Amway Corporation, Ada, Michigan

The goals of the Free Enterprise Institute are three: first, explain and reinforce the reciprocal relationship between personal and economic freedom; second, serve as a clearinghouse for information on free enterprise, bringing together individuals, groups, and organizations sharing a common belief in freedom; third, aid in the creation of rational, responsible citizens aware of their personal roles in the culture which should support limited government.

Underlying these goals is the belief that free enterprise functions as a single element of a larger system -- human freedom itself. Free enterprise is more than an economic theory -- it is the economic dimension of liberty. Economics education involves

more than the teaching of economic principles. Rather, economics education stresses the iron link between personal and economic freedom in a complex world where cultural, economic,
political, and social forces constantly interact. Without both
personal and economic freedom, a truly free society collapses.

FEI's programs consist of the following: (1) a National
Teachers Economic Education Workshop Program; (2) the Institute publishes and distributes the *Free Enterprise Resource
Index*; (3) audiovisual materials in a variety of formats are available on a free-loan basis to educational institutions, service
groups, and individuals; (4) a packet of information on free enterprise is available free of charge; (5) Amway and the Free Enterprise Institute support secondary school and college programs
such as Project Business and Students in Free Enterprise.

The Fraser Institute (FI), Vancouver, British Columbia

FI is an independent Canadian-based economics and social
research and educational organization. Its objective is the redi-
rection of public attention to the role of competitive markets in
providing for the well-being of Canadians. Where markets work,
FI's interest is in trying to discover prospects for application and
expansion of their use. Where markets do not work, FI's interest
lies in finding the reasons for their failure. Where competitive
markets have been replaced by government control, the interest
of FI lies in documenting objectively the nature of the improvement or deterioration resulting from government intervention.

FI seeks to accomplish its objectives by improving the understanding of economic principles and how they apply in practice by
publishing the works of academics and other scholars in a readable yet authoritative and scholarly way. It further seeks to make
these results available to the widest possible audience, both
among the general public and more specialized audiences, such
as students in universities and their teachers, the clergy, and
opinion leaders. Finally, the Institute engages in a wide-range of
community relations projects throughout Canada, involving its
staff in television, radio, and other media activities.

The Fisher Institute (FID), Dallas, Texas

The ultimate aim of the Fisher Institute is to improve the quality of life. A key to this is to teach everyone economics -- how business works, because business is the agency for the organization of production. Economics is important because it is the science of that part of human nature that is predictable. According to FID, an understanding of economics by the majority of Americans is part of the human equation that has been missing through all of mankind's history.

Foundation for Research in Economics and Education (FREE), Lake Jackson, Texas

The goal of FREE is a transformation of public opinion away from a predilection for pervasive government regulation of economic life toward a desire for greater reliance on market determination of economic progress. There are three basic approaches: first, a direct appeal to people's sentiments -- advocacy of a direct, immediate kind with no attempt at presenting objective analysis or fact; second, a presentation of business and economic facts; third, the teaching of economics principles encompassing a set of scientifically verifiable theorems that explain how people behave in the economic sphere. These theories demonstrate how the millions of diverse activities of sellers and consumers of goods and services and owners and users of resources are coordinated and controlled. The third and most important approach is to improve economics teaching in the schools. FREE firmly believes that people who gain an understanding of an economic system will, more than likely, appreciate and defend it.

The Foundation for Teaching Economics (FTE), San Francisco, California

The FTE produces a wide variety of materials including teachers' guides, books, videos and tapes, all designed to improve instruction in economics and entrepreneurship for junior high and high school students. In addition, the Foundation has been actively involved in research in economics education. Beginning in 1991, the FTE will institute a direct instructional seminar on the American economy for young leaders and select teachers.

The FTE's mission statement reads as follows:

The purpose of the Foundation for Teaching Economics is to foster an understanding of the American economic system and the importance of the individual within that system. Through education, the Foundation seeks to prepare young people, selected for their leadership potential, to become economically literate voters, wise consumers and productive citizens of our society.

To carry out this mission, FTE has adopted the following goals:

1. To encourage the teaching of economics in the pre-college curriculum.

2. To develop pre-college programs and educational materials describing the production, distribution, and consumption of goods and services in a free enterprise system.

3. To identify and develop programs and educational materials to train young leaders to be knowledgeable about our economic system and to help economics instructors be more effective teachers.

4. To achieve nationwide distribution and use of these programs and materials.

[Editor's Note: The Foundation for Teaching Economics has been in the process of reorganization during the summer of 1990. Therefore, these mission and goals reflect the organization's expectations rather than current activities.]

The Institute for Humane Studies (IHS), George Mason University, Fairfax, Virginia

The product of the Institute is a continually expanding group of scholars and opinion makers dedicated to a society of free and responsible citizens. IHS's objective is the discovery, development, and placement of scholars and others who deal in ideas that contribute to the intellectual defense of the free society. Everything IHS does serves that objective because its board, officers, and contributors believe that only by changing the academic and intellectual attitude toward individual liberty, private property, and the free market can society be rededicated to these values.

The IHS does not see itself as a think tank but as a "people tank." They do not themselves develop the ideas that will favorably influence the climate of opinion toward liberty; rather, they discover, develop, support, and work with scholars who in turn develop those ideas. IHS begins to work with their scholars during their undergraduate years and continues right through the time when they become tenured professors or pursue other intellectual careers. The IHS provides seminars, scholarships, fellowships, and grants to support scholarship. It also supports a speakers' bureau of its scholars who are available for public presentation.

Their formal programs are only the tip of the iceberg. Perhaps more important are the Institute's formal network of scholars worldwide and IHS's ability to provide key career advice.

Joint Council on Economic Education (JCEE), New York, New York

The JCEE reflects a combined effort of business, labor, agriculture, and education to improve the economic literacy of students through the elementary and secondary grades. The JCEE is a network consisting of a national office, fifty state councils on economics education, and almost three-hundred university-based centers for economics education. Its primary focus is on teacher training and more than 120,000 teachers per year avail themselves of its programs. In addition, the JCEE is extensively involved in developing new materials and curricula for use in the nation's classrooms.

One of its more successful projects has been the developmental economics education program where school districts make commitments to revise their curricula to include economics (K-12th grade) and to provide for teacher training. Over forty percent of the nation's students are now enrolled in developmental economics education program districts. Within the Joint Council network, the statewide councils generate private and public resources to support programming, while the university-based centers deliver the teacher education and provide consultation with individual school districts and their teachers.

The JCEE envisions its mission as increasing and enhancing the quality of all U.S. students' economic understanding. The JCEE believes that this can best be accomplished by helping teachers and, through them, their students to understand more fully the basic attributes and accomplishments of our economic system. The principle way this is to be done is through a trained teacher presenting key economics concepts at the appropriate grade level in an exciting and innovative way. The result is students who have a greater understanding of the U.S. economic system, how to participate effectively in that system, and how to use economic analysis to understand economic, political, and social issues. The Joint Council is the largest, nongovernmental educational delivery system in the world.

Junior Achievement (JA), Colorado Springs, Colorado

Junior Achievement is a seventy-year-old organization that produces a variety of curriculum products to be used at the elementary, intermediate, and secondary level to teach economics to school children. JA works through over 270 franchises throughout the United States that sell their materials to local businesses which, in turn, donate them to the schools. Over a million students were enrolled in classrooms where JA materials were used in 1989. JA stresses the partnership between business and education. JA materials are taught, not only by teachers but by consultants, people from the business community, and others who actually go into the classroom and teach the material and serve as resource people. In addition, JA's after-school program allows high school students an out-of-class opportunity to start their own companies, manufacture, and market a product. The best student businesses are recognized at the National Student Achievement Conference each year.

The Liberty Fund (LI), Indianapolis, Indiana

The Liberty Fund is a tax-exempt privately operated foundation that conducts its own programs and educational activities. It encourages exploration of the nature of man, human freedom, and those institutional arrangements that support liberty. The Liberty Fund is interested in ideas and the refinement of ideas that relate to freedom. The Fund is not an activist organization and does not support action programs. It sponsors seminars, publications, and films designed to promote inquiry into the various aspects of freedom.

The National Center for Privatization (NCP), Wichita, Kansas

The National Center for Privatization has a threefold mission: first, to educate the public on the possibilities of privatization, especially in the Great Plains region; second, to be a player in the preparation of the legislative groundwork for the privatization revolution in public services that is to come; and third, to act as a catalyst in bringing needs, resources, and public support together in the implementation of privatization projects.

The National Center for Policy Analysis (NCPA), Dallas, Texas

The NCPA is a nonprofit, nonpartisan public policy research institute whose purpose is to identify and encourage the best economic research and analysis on major public issues; to make the results of this research known to the general public, the business community, and policymakers; and to focus public attention on private alternatives to government regulation and control.

NCPA describes itself as a think tank that supports free enterprise, low taxes, limited government, and a secure national defense.

NCPA's main vehicle is a continuing series of policy reports. While research-based, these are written for public, not academic, presentation. NCPA's reports usually receive widespread coverage in the media.

The National Schools Committee for Economic Education (NSCEE), Cos Cob, Connecticut

This organization believes that economics education should teach young people the values of the free-market system. In the NSCEE's view, the free-market system is the most vital and beneficial economic system. The NSCEE does not object to a comparative approach that allows students to learn about other economic systems.

The NSCEE tries to achieve its goals by offering simplified, yet useful strategies and materials for teaching economics. Their approach is that instruction which is focused on concepts, words, and phrases is the most effective way of helping people understand economics.

Securities Industry Foundation for Economic Education (SIF), New York, New York

SIF's program begins with the proposition that economics impacts all Americans. It is the cornerstone of the U.S. democratic and capitalist society. Economics is the bridge between hopes and reality. Yet it remains to most Americans an invisible science.

The members of the Securities Industry Foundation seek to be looked upon and called upon to act as capitalist spokesmen. They see a major opportunity and responsibility to provide economic leadership and to stand and be counted as individuals who believe in a free capitalistic society. The Foundation believes in sharing this information with fellow Americans.

SIF sees the problem faced by the U.S. as the economic illiteracy of the voters in this country. The securities industry must take a role in combating this ignorance, for the industry is dependent for success on a broad understanding of the economic system.

The Foundation lists its objectives as follows: first, to foster economics understanding of the American system of free enterprise and, by so doing, encourage a broader recognition of a vital role played in this system by the securities industry; second, to carry on, assist, and contribute to the support of economics educational activities and products; third, to assist and contribute to the support of economics education organizations; and four, to assist, support, organize, or otherwise promote the involvement of securities industry leaders and personnel in such economics education activities, products, and organizations.

THE CASES AGAINST
ECONOMICS EDUCATION

Michael Watts

The traditional, content-based case for economics education programs, which the critics discussed in this paper oppose, has been made by noted U.S. economists for at least a century. Consider the following statements by three former presidents of the American Economic Association:

> The [social and economic] revolution now in progress is making every man and every woman an economist. . . . The economists who are thus being made are, it must be admitted, just now pretty poor ones. . . . But it is a great thing to have the whole nation at school in political economy. (Francis A. Walker 1891.)

> [T]hat the public does concern itself most frequently with economic questions . . . is a true and persuasive reason for its possessing economic literacy. In the best of all worlds it might be most desirable to have musical or theological literacy, but in ours the public wants to talk about money. Although the public cannot have universal literacy, that is no reason for possessing no special knowledge at all. The public has chosen to speak and vote on economic problems, so the only question is how intelligently it speaks and votes. (George J. Stigler 1970.)

> My goals and objectives in teaching the Principles [of economics] . . . are to initiate students in a basic understanding of the economy and the tools of economics that make this possible. . . . [Y]ou can't have one without the other. (Robert Eisner 1990.)

Given this consistent and long-standing concern with economic literacy by prominent leaders of the economics profession, one might think that this "standard" case for economics education programs would be widely accepted by other economists and academics as self-evident. But in fact, the content-literacy case for economics education is much harder to sell, even to many educators and some economists, than Jefferson and Locke's inalienable rights of life, liberty, and the pursuit of happiness or property.

Some of the critics who reject the standard case for economics education are openly hostile to the basic idea of providing such programs in the nation's schools. Others provisionally accept the general goal of promoting economic literacy in some format(s), but chastise certain attributes or objectives of mainstream economics education programs as they are currently practiced. Both types of objections, general and limited, have been made by both orthodox and dissident economists, by similarly divergent academics from other subject areas, and by nonacademic observers of the U.S. educational system. Political liberals, moderates, and conservatives are all well represented among the orthodox critics.

Whenever such a diverse group of writers -- and particularly academics -- agrees about anything, it is informative to consider which specific points in their arguments are held in common, and which are not. It is also useful to assess how telling their critiques have been in reshaping the programs that are criticized and, conversely, how successful other practitioners in the area subject to the criticism have been in responding to those challenges. That is the focus of this review, which is organized around three major charges that have been leveled against economics education programs in the U.S. in recent decades: (1) ideological bias, (2) misdirected focus or content, and (3) private versus public good aspects of economics education.

Charges of Ideological Bias

Many who condemn or criticize economics education programs claim that the programs represent a fundamentally corrupt exercise in defending the status quo, and serve as an apologia for the powerful interests of big business or old money. Socialists such as Edward Bellamy have long popularized this view in attacks on the orthodox economics profession itself (see Bellamy's satirical "Parable of the Water Tank," for example), and similar charges have been lodged by those who are merely anti-business rather than pro-socialist.

One noteworthy example of the ideological-bias critique was published in the Winter 1979 issue of *The Insurgent Sociologist*, and directed against the nation's largest economics education organization, the Joint Council on Economic Education (JCEE). Karl Kreplin claimed that

in reality economic education is a method by which the American upper class attempts to legitimate the American system of monopoly capitalism. . . . [It] tries to promote an ideology aimed at defending the existing economic system and at reproducing existing class relations. (Kreplin 1979, 3)

Several social studies education professors have echoed that attack, and a few have even extended it to textbook publishers and authors in the area of economics education, not just to organizations like the JCEE and Junior Achievement which are seen as inherently suspect because they accept and solicit major funding from business organizations and foundations. (For example, Kreplin devotes half a page in his article to a partial listing of JCEE funders -- including the Committee for Economic Development, the American Bankers Association, the American Petroleum Institution, both major stock exchanges, the National Association of Manufacturers, the U.S. Chamber of Commerce, the Ford Foundation, and the Alfred P. Sloan Foundation -- and to organizations which have helped to plan its programs or, through their executives, offered endorsements for the JCEE's efforts -- including AT&T, the President's Council of Economic Advisers, the National Bureau of Economic Research, the Brookings Institute, and Resources for the Future. Kreplin doesn't mention the AFL-CIO and other labor organizations for some reason, though they also provide funding and board members for the JCEE.)

The most strident article attacking textbook authors and publishers was written by Bruce R. Romanish, and published in a 1983 article of *Theory and Research in Social Education*, the journal of the College and University Faculty Association of the National Council for the Social Studies.

After reviewing ten texts, Romanish concluded that, as a group, the books

> **present an explanation of economic constructs that is harmonious with the existing economic order in America. . . . The bias is accented by . . . a 'this is the way it is' approach. . . . [T]hey present free enterprise principles to the exclusion of other ideas.** (Romanish 1983, 18)

But Romanish's "facts," procedures, and conclusions were sharply challenged in a "Response" article published in the same journal (Walstad and Watts 1984). Writing as self-professed mainstream economic educators, these respondents claimed to show that Romanish's work contained numerous errors and offered "strong assertions, no proof, little evidence, and a flawed and inconsistent framework for analysis" (Walstad and Watts 1984, 35). Then, in a later article, Watts (1987) contrasted the positivist methodology that is accepted by most economists to that adopted by Romanish and many other social studies educators. These educators' methodology holds that

> **any attempt at separation of ideology from economic education is fraudulent. Economics, far from being truth, involves ideologies, some of which are contradictory and competing. Furthermore, the form and nature of education are ideological at their base.** (Nelson and Carlson 1985)

Such a view of economics and education leads to a basic difference in recommended educational practices, particularly in the social sciences, when compared to the positivist methodology that dominates economic thought and textbooks at both the college and pre-college levels. Economists see it as largely pointless to label all education and educational thought as ideologically driven or biased, and call for extensive instruction on concepts and factual material which they accept as "value free," even when those concepts and facts are used to analyze and evaluate (in a cost-benefit framework) public-policy proposals that are explicitly aimed at reaching some values-based goals.

The "ideology-everywhere" educators favor devoting much more classroom time and discussion to the personal and social goals that underlie public policy, the factors which determine those goals, and cross-cultural comparisons of goals and other normative issues. Mainstream economists respond by pointing out that, time and time again, public policies which are established to achieve some stated goal have unexpected and perverse effects because they are so often adopted without adequate attention to positive economic relationships and evidence. Economists also choose to focus more attention on the process of voluntary exchange between private producers and consumers, which raises fewer public-policy questions to be debated in terms of particular laws and regulations designed to achieve a specific goal. (The broader issue of how much time to spend comparing alternative types of economic systems is discussed in the following section.)

While it is theoretically possible that, given sufficient time and face-to-face discussion, the positivist economists could come to an agreement with the educators who see ideology on every page of economics and education textbooks or in other curriculum materials, it is at least equally likely that both groups would view this debate as one involving absolute statements of truth, faith, or time-proven rules, which neither camp is prepared to concede. And it is even more likely that the costs of bringing the two groups together on these points would far exceed any benefits, assuming it is eventually possible to reach such an accord.

Nevertheless, the two groups do have more in common than most of their representatives may suspect. Their major point of agreement in terms of economics education practices and materials is an inherent skepticism about the supposedly altruistic behaviors of most, if not all, special-interest groups which sponsor and support these initiatives. This is, in fact, an old tradition among both groups; in the case of economists, it literally dates back at least to Adam Smith. Far from being the unswerving representative of business interests he is sometimes claimed to be, in 1776 Smith wrote that "People of the same trade seldom meet together, even for merriment and diversion, but the conversation ends in a conspiracy against the public, or in some contrivance to raise prices" (Smith 1776, 144). While Smith more often discussed merchants, manufacturers and other particular business groups as productive but self-seeking individuals or groups, note that in this passage he used a broader category -- "people of the same trade" -- which applies to educators as fully as it does to business or labor representatives. I will return to this point in a later section.

Among the education professors who have attacked biased economics materials in the classroom and the special-interest forces that put them there, none has been more direct or forceful than M. L. Frankel, who wrote the following words near the end of his long tenure (1955-77) as the first president of the Joint Council:

> Neatly packaged, beautifully prepared with detailed teacher instructions, closed-ended and directed to achieve an a priori objective of the producer, overwhelming amounts of materials and programs are offered free and in quantity by literally thousands of organizations representing members from all walks of life. For example, in an evaluation of written materials in economics other than texts produced by such organizations ostensibly for use in the schools, (an) examining committee of scholars found that only 40 percent of 5,000 items were considered usable in the schools. . . . Well-reasoned policy positions have their place in the classroom if. . . they are presented as one of many alternative solutions and not as the ultimate truth. But outright propaganda, half-truth, and misinformation does not.
>
> Much of what flows into the schools is sheer propaganda and avowedly produced for that purpose. Other material has advertising as its objective. Still others are outright policy statements without being so labeled . . . .
>
> Pressures are often placed on superintendents of schools to accept materials that have been produced by noneducational organizations. In one case, such an organization produced a series of films, a flip-board, and a small text for use in the schools. These materials were anything but objective and contained considerable misinformation. . . . The procedure of getting these into the schools was to visit several corporate executives in a

community and convince them how important these materials would be for the schools and that the company should sponsor for a price the complete set for the school. The agent then visited the superintendent and conveyed the message to him that a company had purchased these materials for the school and they were to be used in the classroom. Conscious of his community relations, the superintendent expressed gratification for the gift. . . . The regular class program was interrupted to accommodate the materials. And an injustice was done to education. (Frankel 1976, 7)

Frankel goes on to consider similarly self-interested and one-sided materials and curriculum programs sponsored by government agencies, labor unions, and teachers' own professional associations. But apart from extending his discussion to non-business organizations, his concerns are quite similar to those raised by other educators and journalists, ranging from the very conservative to the very liberal. See, for example, Matthew Lyon's "Buying into the Public Schools: And now The Word from our sponsor" (1978), Fred Hechinger's "The Corporation in the Classroom" (1978), Irving Kristol's "On 'Economic Education'" (1978), and Sheila Harty's *Hucksters in the Classroom: A Review of Industry Propaganda in Schools* (1979).

The problem of ideological bias in special-interest materials is a particularly serious one in economics education because of the comparatively low levels of teacher training in this subject area (see Walstad and Watts 1985); the large number of schools which have no formal requirements in the subject area, and so rely on K-12 "infusion" approaches for economics education despite indications from both teachers and students that they often find economics a hard and boring, although important, subject; and finally, as noted by Frankel and the others cited earlier, the sheer number of organizations which have a particular message to sell related to some set of current or proposed economic policies.

To summarize, the broad complaint that mainstream economics and/or economics education programs are or must be ideologically based is rejected out of hand by most economists and economic educators, even while they accept the claim that some instructional materials, authors and institutions may suffer from

111

exactly that kind of problem. That leaves two other, albeit more limited, charges against economics education programs to review. Significantly, these more limited complaints are often made by noted economic educators.

Misdirected Focus or Content

Among those who accept the idea that economics education is important and not inherently flawed by ideological bias, there are still many who argue that current economics education practices and materials are poorly conceived or delivered. These critics can be divided into three groups:

- Those who call for more attention to international concepts, issues, and comparisons of alternative economic systems.

- Those who push for a fundamental focus on decision-making skills in all, or nearly all, economics education programs.

- Those who call for greater emphasis on citizenship education, particularly at the pre-college level.

This classification is, of course, merely an expository convenience -- some individuals can, and do, advocate two or all three of these positions simultaneously.

International content and comparisons

At both the college and pre-college levels, many economists have recently attacked textbooks and teachers for skimping on coverage of international economics. That complaint was frequently heard at two conferences recently sponsored by the JCEE and is recorded in proceedings volumes published as special issues of the *Journal of Economic Education*. The first conference was held at MIT and featured critiques of Part I of the JCEE's *Master Curriculum Guide* (see Highsmith and Kasper 1987); the second conference, sponsored by Purdue University to discuss textbooks for college-level principles of economics courses, includes responses by a group of prominent textbook authors (see Bartlett and Weidenaar 1988). Two research articles have recently provided data which support claims that coverage of international concepts and issues has been relatively limited both in college principles of economics textbooks (Walstad and Watts 1990) and in high school social studies classes (Watts and High-smith 1990). In the last few years, however, college textbook authors and publishers have scrambled to expand, emphasize, and market their coverage of international concepts and topics. At the pre-college level teachers' limited training in economics and the slower revision and adoption cycles for textbooks makes this a more difficult problem to address.

Many of the complaints offered at the JCEE conferences were simply statements to the effect that, since international trade and finance issues have become a major feature of daily life for U.S. consumers, workers, and firms and play a large role in public-policy debates, the instructors, authors, and publishers should reflect that new reality in their classroom materials and activities. But more sweeping and shrill complaints were also heard. Romanish, for example, pointed to the limited coverage of alternative economic systems in high school economics textbooks as a reflection of ideological bias. More moderately, in a review of a similar (partly overlapping) set of high school textbooks, Suzanne Wiggins Helburn concluded that

> to some extent [the textbooks] only pay lip service to the free enterprise orientation, and provide fairly standard, if highly simplified, viewpoints of the subject. . . .
>
> Overwhelmingly, the books provide a consensual lens and an officially defined interpretation of reality -- entirely within the accepted neoclassical tradition. . . .
>
> [N]one of the books consider as problematic the basic concepts and social vision of mainstream economics. Except for the occasional brief biography of Keynes or Galbraith, the only alternative school of thought which is mentioned is Marxism, which is usually introduced as a foil, not as a serious world view. . . . [S]tudents in the U.S. are learning basic concepts from the neoclassical paradigm as a catechism; to a lesser extent, they are learning to use these concepts to understand the profes-

sion's view of basic economic policy controversy. . . .
[T]he JCEE Framework and the diffusion of its content in
the curriculum via textbooks is a real tribute to the profession's 'maturity' and 'normality' in Katouzian's (methodological) sense of the word. (Helburn 1986, 26, 28, 29)

Several counterarguments have been presented by economists (especially textbook authors) to explain why more cannot be
done, or at least had not been done, with international economics
at the college and pre-college levels. For example, Campbell
McConnell noted at the 1987 Purdue conference that

In general, a meaningful discussion of international
economics and finance presumes that the student already has a fair grasp of micro and macro theory. I am
fairly confident that this is the basic reason that international trade and finance constitute the closing chapters
of most textbooks; it is not because of the failure of
textbook authors to appreciate the increasing importance of the topic. (McConnell 1988, 149)

Walstad and Watts (1984) point out that for precollege students familiarity with domestic institutions may also be a prerequi-
site for understanding international agencies and arrangements
and, at least in the U.S., that the share of national income that is
directly determined through international trade activities is still
relatively small when compared to the aggregate level of domestic
consumption, investment, and government spending. Secondary
students typically take only a one-semester course in economics,
or none at all, so in the limited time that is allocated to their
economics instruction, it may well be reasonable to spend most
time on national rather than on international material.

In a recent survey of U.S. secondary social studies teachers,
however, it was shown that some classroom time is already being
spent on the general topics of international economic institutions
and issues (Watts and Highsmith 1990). The problem is that the
current lessons include little or no coverage of basic economic
concepts, such as comparative advantage and exchange-rate
adjustments, which are used to analyze the international topics
and issues regularly presented in the media. So while today's
high school students may be learning more about what is happen-

ing in the international arena, they appear to learn very little about the causes or consequences of these events.

On the narrower issue of teaching comparative economic systems, the critics of mainstream practice have made much less headway. Specialized courses in this area are not widely required, even for economics majors at the college level (Siegfried and Wilkinson 1982). The studies of introductory textbooks at the college and pre-college levels, noted earlier, report fairly limited coverage on this topic, with no coverage at all included in some of the texts. And finally, the recent movement to more capitalistic forms of organization in the Soviet Union and many nations in Eastern Europe raises new questions about the importance of teaching U.S. students about strict systems of central planning. With often-dissident economists such as Robert Heilbroner declaring openly that capitalism has won its economic "war" with socialism, at least for the time being, there is a natural tendency to see instruction on the proper role and scope of government in a mixed-market economy as more relevant and important than lessons on the older issues of comparative economic systems (in the sense of comparing and contrasting capitalism and socialism), or alternative systems of economic thought such as Marxism.

Decision-making skills

Helburn also laments the lack of emphasis on "student practice in decision making" (Helburn 1986, 27), but on this count her criticism is surpassed in fervor, frequency, and length by some members of the JCEE's own national network of state councils and college and university centers for economics education. Beverly Armento (1987), for example, recently described the educational and psychological research on problem solving and offered several basic recommendations for using this approach to teach economics. But the most outspoken advocate of "reasoning" or decision-making skills as the ultimate rationale for economics education -- and at the same time the leading critic of many existing programs and materials because, in his opinion, they lack this feature -- is Donald Wentworth (1987). Typical classroom practices and typical economics lessons, as Wentworth describes them in a classic strawman depiction, involve rote learning and drill-and-practice sessions that are essentially no different from the satirical lecture on the Smoot-Hawley tariffs in the movie *Ferris Bueller's Day Off.* Wentworth believes that:

economic education suffers from the problem of mediocre teaching and student disengagement endemic to all social science education in our schools. . . .

A curriculum focus on economic reasoning could help improve instruction and promote student interest if economic educators are guided by three important guidelines or reminders:

First, learning economic content will not necessarily contribute to improving students' ability to reason economically.

Second, the assumptions and skills necessary to accomplish economic reasoning can be taught and used well before students possess a great knowledge of economic content.

Third, instruction in economic reasoning should be given a higher priority than instruction in economic content. (Wentworth 1987, 175)

Wentworth's agenda has influenced national economics education efforts at the pre-college level in at least one explicit result: a JCEE publication entitled *Developing Reasoning as the Fourth R* (Dawson 1982). And Ron VanSicle (1990) now goes so far as to declare victory for the decision-making emphasis: "Economic educators agree that the primary goal of economics education is to teach students to reason effectively with economic knowledge in their public and private lives." There is, in fact, clearly some support for such a claim.

At the college and university level, for example, many of the same concerns with reasoning and decision making are reflected in a set of papers which criticize researchers in economics education for relying predominantly, if not exclusively, on standardized, objective test scores as the basic measure of output in economics coursework. That literature is briefly reviewed in Siegfried and Walstad (1990), and lies behind some recent work on the struc-

116

ture of the undergraduate economics major which was funded as part of an American Association of Colleges project to investigate outcomes expected from "study-in-depth" in various subject areas. In a draft of the paper on the economics major from this series, the authors complain that "The [current] focus on coverage of content is inconsistent with the goals of the major" (Siegfried et. al. 1989, 14), which they identify as an emphasis on deductive reasoning; building and using parsimonious models; knowledge of universal economic principles; familiarity with decision-making tools such as examining trade-offs, comparing opportunity costs, constrained maximization procedures, and various efficiency concepts; an interest in testing predictions from abstract theoretical models; and the ability to use data and statistical methods or tests.

The traditional, content-based case for economics education is, of course, not always or necessarily at odds with decision-making oriented activities and materials. Indeed, if cost-benefit analysis is viewed as synonymous with the notion of decision making in economic contexts, the disagreement is largely defined away and boils down to the more narrowly pedagogical issue of how much time to spend on applications and "real-world" demonstrations of concepts and models versus the instructional reinforcement that can be achieved by covering a wider range of models and concepts. However, it is also clear that many economists would maintain their primary focus on a content-based case for economics education even if other subjects (such as logic, math, computer science, or other social sciences) are someday proven conclusively to be more effective in improving students' general decision-making skills. And furthermore, as cognitive psychologists have identified a larger part of the decision-making process as domain-specific, involving discipline-based "schematic" and "conditional" knowledge as well as basic facts and concepts, and as they have come to describe domain-specific procedures as "strong" knowledge when compared to the general cognitive strategies that are "weak in the sense that they do not depend on much domain-specific knowledge and do not lead to solutions with as much certainty as more domain-specific procedures often do" (VanSicle 1990, 10), the case for a primary emphasis on domain-specific knowledge and procedures has been strengthened.

117

There is also a set of research results which is at least tangentially related to this particular discussion (see Walstad, 1987). For years, some economic educators argued that teachers at all grade levels should design lessons and activities that are active, entertaining and obviously "relevant" to students' lives, so that students will like economics and their coursework more and, *as a result*, learn more economics. But others argued that those who learn more economics will, other things being equal, be those who tend to enjoy the subject more. The result was a classic chicken-and-egg debate: which comes first, liking economics or learning it? Fortunately, that question is something economic educators can model and measure, and results from several studies that looked at both sides of this process showed consistently that causation runs from learning economics to liking it, *not vice versa*.

To summarize, the debate over reasoning and decision making has led to much the same sort of outcome as the calls for greater emphasis on international concepts and issues. The mainstream, content-based case has been stretched to incorporate a substantial part of what these critics wanted to see done, at least in terms of statements on the goals of college and pre-college economics education. But the central emphasis on discipline-specific concepts and, as Keynes described it, "the *economic way of thinking*" (my emphasis) has been little affected in practical and measurable terms, such as limiting the scope of what key concepts, models and empirical facts are designated as basic parts of standard curriculum materials. Those who call for a further emphasis on reasoning, to the point of imposing restrictions on the content or quantity of content that is taught, are seen as reformers promoting a special cause in the economics education movement and are not dismissed as intolerable heretics.

Better citizenship through economics education

There is an extensive academic literature, written primarily by social studies education professors and pre-college social studies teachers affiliated with the National Council for the Social Studies, arguing that the case for all social studies education, including economics education, must be based on the need for an active and well-informed citizenry in democratic nations such as the U.S. An NCSS Task Force on Scope and Sequence which offered recommendations for K-12 plans of study in the social studies provided the following rationale for citizenship education:

> **Citizenship means that an individual is fully franchised as a member of a political community. The rights, duties, responsibilities and entitlements embodied in the franchise apply evenhandedly to those who have the abilities and skills needed to participate in the social life of the group. But what becomes of those who do not acquire such abilities and skills? Moreover, can a society that assumes responsible citizen involvement in decision making survive if members do not, will not, or cannot participate in such decision making?** (NCSS 1984, 250)

The JCEE reprints this paragraph in its own scope and sequence document (Gilliard et. al. 1988. 3), and regularly promotes the need to improve students' economic understanding to help them in their roles as consumers, producers and voters. The citizenship argument for economics education was even popular enough to make its way into the only consensus statement of goals for economics education that was formally developed from, and subsequently supported by, survey responses from practicing economists, educators and economics educators (Horton and Weidenaar 1975). But those surveys also showed that there were some members of these professions who strongly opposed this (and other) arguments for economics education. So it was no great surprise when, in 1977, Richard McKenzie raised a stern challenge for the citizenship advocates in an article entitled "Where Is the Economics in Economic Education?"

McKenzie argued that individuals won't voluntarily learn economics just to improve the quality of citizenship, because the private returns in doing so are insufficient to offset the costs of becoming and remaining economically literate. Even if the benefits were that high, McKenzie argued, it would not be economically sensible for many individuals to take the time and trouble to vote using this knowledge. Also, he noted, voters are most likely to support the candidates and propositions that are most favorable to the voters' own private interests, regardless of what the voters know about the overall social merits of some proposal or candidate. And finally, McKenzie wrote, "If the ultimate objective of economic education is to produce a 'better citizenry,' then we must ask what a better citizenry is and how [it] can be produced." (1977, 10) Public choice theory has shown that answering such questions in a democratic environment is fraught with difficulties and inconsistencies, so McKenzie concluded that

> **we must ask some tough questions. Do voters really have sufficient incentive to become and remain economically literate and to employ what they know in the political process? Economics is one of a number of subjects which have potential external benefits. Assuming that students cannot learn everything, what claim does economic education have on public resources relative to other subjects? Can we argue for the introduction of economic education without opening up the public school curriculum to exploitation by all interest groups who believe that their subjects rightfully have greater claim to resources than economics?**

Robert Horton and Leonard Martin published comments on McKenzie's article in 1979. Horton strongly agreed with McKenzie's critique of the citizenship goal and the problems associated with public-good questions concerning economics education. But he argued that McKenzie was addressing issues that dealt primarily with "advanced courses" in economics, not "economics education 'as a matter of general education.'" His own focus on general education led Horton to see the consumers of economics education as "not just students, but also parents, community members, and others" (Horton 1979, 31). And in that sense Horton saw many private good aspects to economics education and general education because

> **After all, communities do display rivalries in their school systems; parents do purchase independent education for themselves and for their children; and administrators, curriculum specialists, and teachers do differentiate their products.** (1979, 31)

Martin agreed that

Education is essentially a private good and surely not a pure public good. It is not indivisible and it does not become a free good to all others as soon as it has been acquired by one person. Thus, it is not education which is a public good, but rather citizenship. (1979, 28)

What this exchange makes clear is that, although many social studies educators would like to make economics education a key part of the citizenship education movement and view content-based arguments for instruction on economics and other social sciences as incomplete or misdirected, economists are often uncomfortable with such initiatives and fundamentally skeptical about the potential effectiveness of any citizenship education programs. The issue of public versus private good aspects of economics education, and education in general, is more complex and discussed at greater length in the following section.

Economics Education as a Private Versus a Public Good

If knowing economics is something people want to do because they enjoy it, or because it makes them better off by allowing them to make better decisions as consumers, workers, or investors, they will be willing and able to pay for course work, instructional materials, and economic information provided by sellers who derive pleasure or income by producing these services. That establishes a private market for economics education that, if it is competitive, will efficiently allocate scarce resources to these pursuits. In equilibrium, the marginal private benefit of the last unit of economics education services produced will be equal to the marginal private cost of producing them. If all of the costs and benefits associated with this production are private in the sense of falling to the producers and consumers of these services, there is no economic reason for public intervention that will lead to changes in the market-determined price or quantity of these services.

Many people argue, however, that some benefits of general education, and economics education in particular, fall to third parties who are not direct producers or consumers of these products. These external or spillover benefits are thought to come in such forms as lower unemployment and crime rates and in related decreases in public expenditures for welfare and other assistance or retraining programs. For economics education, the argument is often made that workers will make fewer unreasonable demands of their employers or that there will be greater "pressure for better [public] policies" (Martin 1979, 28) if the public's levels of economic understanding are improved. Businesses that support economics education programs are thus seen as promoting their own interests in one (economic rather than ideological) sense, but as G.L. Bach (1979) of Stanford University pointed out bluntly in his article on "Economic Education and America's Love-Hate Affair with Big Business," that an economically literate population is not one which will always adopt a pro--business stance, nor will economics education alone be sufficient "to provide the legitimacy so essential to business firms if they are to play their role effectively at the center of a market-directed economy" (Bach 1979, 7).

There is an extensive, often-debated, and on many counts inconclusive literature on the rate of return to public expenditures for general education (see Ehrenberg and Smith 1988, 319-325 for a brief summary). Returns appear to be higher in less developed countries than in wealthier nations, and higher for spending on pre-college expenditures than for spending on higher education. Certain areas of education (such as mechanics and engineering) are also thought to have a stronger and more certain effect on national productivity levels than others. No empirical study has appeared to date which estimates productivity gains or other financial returns associated with improved levels of economic understanding, and the measurement problems in trying to develop such estimates are severe.

But there is another type of market failure that does suggest a role for public policy initiatives which expand and enhance economics education programs in the nation's schools. This argument has to do with the assumption, made earlier, that the market for economics education is competitive. At least at the pre-college level, this is clearly not the case.

Most pre-college students attend public schools, and in recent decades public schools and school districts have grown much larger due to population growth during the baby-boom period, perceived economies of scale in school operations, and curriculum and administrative pressures for greater specialization and division of labor among professional and administrative staffs. In terms of curriculum and course design, these trends have led to greater centralization at the state and school district levels, which was further supported by the evolution of schools and departments of education at colleges and universities around the nation. Today, to get a position as a pre-college classroom teacher or administrator, the relevant licensing requirement is a degree in education, not a degree in economics or other "pure content" areas such as English or mathematics. Many economists have argued that this structure is inherently inefficient as a model for providing general education -- for example, see *The Public School Monopoly* (Everhart 1982). In terms of providing appropriate kinds and levels of economics education, it creates several special problems.

First, even pre-college teachers and administrators who specialize in the social studies have little or no formal training in economics (see Walstad and Watts 1985, and Watts 1986 and 1989). That clearly lowers their ability to deliver such training, and quite probably their interest in trying to do so in the first place. Second, social studies teachers and administrators are more likely to be extensively trained in history, world history, and geography, and throughout this century have clearly structured the curriculum to stress history (see Peet 1984) and, more recently, history, geography and civics programs which stress the themes of time, place, and citizenship (NCSS 1989). Finally, given broad-based and special-interest pressures to include instruction on current social problems in the curriculum -- in programs such as values, drug, sex, or aids education -- there is widespread opposition to adding any additional content subjects, especially as required courses or as an infusion component in already required courses. Recent emphasis on standardized testing and school or teacher "accountability" usually reinforces this reluctance unless, of course, a "new" subject is well represented on the test instruments used to evaluate educational achievement and performance.

The monopoly argument suggests that, although economics education may be largely or even entirely a private good, there is still a role for intervention in educational markets to weaken or compensate for the barriers to entry that restrict academic training in economics for both students and teachers.

Conclusions

At present, the theoretical argument concerning whether or how much economics education belongs in the schools is primarily a matter of personal belief. Economic educators have empirically demonstrated numerous ways to teach more economics effectively, but there are no hard facts or empirically based estimates of what that learning is worth. The same is true in many other subject areas, of course -- most of what we know about the productivity effects of education relates to very basic skills such as reading, writing, and arithmetic or, at the college and university level, knowledge of how to build tangible goods that is typically acquired in engineering and science programs. Other kinds of education may also enhance productivity, or they may simply help employers identify those who are innately more productive due to intelligence or good work habits and those who are not.

At the pragmatic level of practice and politics, the cases for and against economics education are inevitably weighed by people and organizations with varied interests and backgrounds, often with a personal and even a financial stake in how much, or how little, economics will be included in the curriculum. Citizenship operates as a public good in this context, and public-spirited discussion and essays certainly have their place in these debates. But in the long run it seems most likely that teachers and schools will produce more economics education if that training is specifically recognized and rewarded by the institutions that accept their graduates as employees or as more advanced students.

In the meantime, even without empirical evidence on the economic value of learning in such areas as economics, history, biology, music, and theology, decisions about the composition of the curriculum must be made by educators, parents, and public officials. And on this level there are still two fundamental arguments for economics education:

1. Microeconomics and macroeconomics are major forces which shape, in large part, the modern world. People without formal training in economics regularly exhibit ignorance of basic economic measures such as profits, inflation rates, and patterns of income distribution; systematic misinformation on these and other such measures; and persistent misunderstandings concerning the operations of local, national, and international markets, and the effectiveness, limitations, and long-term consequences of public policy remedies for various economic problems. That ignorance, misinformation, and misunderstanding is at least potentially damaging to the efficient operation of a democratic, market-based economic and political system, even though we do not yet have hard evidence to document the extent or severity of such problems.

2. Applying the basic notion of opportunity cost to current curriculum content and practices suggests that, given the preceding arguments, there are current lessons and full courses which are being offered that have a weaker claim for these scarce resources than does economics education. The cases for many subjects other than economics are not supported by empirical estimates of their ultimate value as consumption or investment goods. Even in courses such as English and mathematics where financial returns are better documented, infusing economics instruction is often both feasible and effective instructional practice (see, for example, Chizmar et. al. 1985; Becker 1990; and Watts and Smith 1989).

It is not surprising that economics educators do not find the cases against economics education compelling. However, reviewing those challenges can help to refine the case statement for special training in economics, and the specific content and structure of the economics education programs that are provided to meet the goals of economic literacy.

REFERENCES

Armento, B. J. 1989. "Ideas for Teaching Economics Derived from Learning Theory." *Theory Into Practice.* (Summer).

Bach, G. L. 1979. "Economic Education and America's Love-Hate Affair with Big Business." *Journal of Economic Education.* (October) special reprint.

Bartlett, R. L. and D. J. Weidenaar. 1988. "An Introduction to the Proceedings of the Invitational Conference on the Principles of Economics Textbook." *Journal of Economic Education.* (Spring).

Becker, W. E. 1990. "The Use of Mathematics and Statistics in the Teaching of Economics." In P. Saunders and W. B. Walstad. eds., *The Principles of Economics Course: A Handbook for Instructors.* New York: McGraw-Hill.

Chizmar, J. F., B. J. McCarney, R. S. Halinski, and M. J. Racich, ed. 1985. "'Give and Take,' Economics Achievement, and Basic Skills Development." *Journal of Economic Education.* (Spring).

Dawson, G. G. 1982 ed. *Developing Reasoning as the Fourth R.* New York: Joint Council on Economic Education.

Ehrenberg, R. G. and R. S. Smith. 1988. *Modern Labor Economics.* Glenview, Illinois: Scott, Foresman and Company.

Eisner, R. 1990. "Learning About Economics and the Economy." In P. Saunders and W. B. Walstad, eds. *The Principles of Economics Course: A Handbook for Instructors.* New York: McGraw-Hill.

Everhart, R. B. 1982 ed. *The Public School Monopoly: A Critical Analysis of Education and the State in American Society.* San Francisco: Pacific Institute for Public Policy Research.

Frankel, M. L. 1976. "Hidden Forces in Education." *UCLA Educator*. (Winter).

Gilliard, J. V., et al. 1988. *Master Curriculum Guide in Economics, Economics: What and When, Scope and Sequence Guidelines*. New York: Joint Council on Economic Education.

Harty, S. 1979. *Hucksters in the Classroom: A Review of Industry Propaganda in the Schools*. Washington, D.C.: Center for the Study of Responsive Law.

Hechinger, F. M. 1978. "The Corporation in the Classroom." *Saturday Magazine*. (16 September).

Helburn, S. W. 1986. "Economics and Economic Education: The Selective Use of Discipline Structures in Economics Curricula." In S. Hodkinson and D. J. Whitehead, eds. *Economics Education: Research and Development Issues*. London: Longman.

Highsmith, R. and H. Kasper. 1987. "Rethinking the Scope of Economics." *Journal of Economic Education*. (Spring).

Horton, R. V. 1979. "Comment on Richard B. McKenzie's 'Where Is the Economics in Economic Education?'" *Journal of Economic Education*. (Fall).

_____ and D. J. Weidenaar. 1975. "Wherefore Economic Education?" *Journal of Economic Education*. (Fall).

Kreplin, K. 1979. "The American Upper Class and the Problem of Legitimacy: The Joint Council on Economic Education." *The Insurgent Sociologist*. (Winter).

Kristol, I., 1978, "On 'Economic Education'." In Kristol's *Two Cheers for Capitalism*. New York: Mentor Press.

Lyon, M. 1978. "Buying Into the Public Schools: And Now The Word From Our Sponsor." *The Texas Observer*. (3 November).

127

Martin, L. W. 1979. "Where Is the Economics in Economic Education? Another View." *Journal of Economic Education.* (Fall).

McConnell, C. R. 1988. "The Principles of Economics Course from Now Until Then: A Response," *Journal of Economic Education.* (Spring).

McKenzie, R. B. 1977. "Where Is the Economics in Economic Education?" *Journal of Economic Education.* (Fall).

NCSS Task Force on Scope and Sequence. 1984. "In Search of Scope and Sequence for Social Studies." *Social Education.* (April).

_____. 1989. "Report of the Ad Hoc Committee on Scope and Sequence," *Social Education.* (October).

Nelson, J. C. and K. Carlson. 1981. "Ideology and Economic Education," In Symmes, ed. *Economic Education: Links to the Social Studies.* Washington, D.C.: National Council for the Social Studies.

Peet, T. S. 1984. "A Selective History of Social Studies Scope and Sequence Patterns, 1916-1984." Ph.D. diss., The Ohio State University, Columbus.

Romanish, B. A. 1983. "Modern Secondary Economics Textbooks and Ideological Bias." *Theory and Research in Social Education.* (Spring).

Siegfried, J. J. et al. 1989. "The Economics Major in American Higher Education," Working paper. (October).

_____ and W. B. Walstad. 1990. "Research on Teaching College Economics." In P. Saunders and W. B. Walstad, eds. *The Principles of Economics Course: A Handbook for Instructors.* New York: McGraw-Hill.

_____ and J. T. Wilkinson. 1982. "The Economics Curriculum in the United States: 1980." *American Economic Review.* (May).

Smith, A. 1976. *An Inquiry Into the Nature and Causes of the Wealth of Nations*. E. Cannan, ed. Chicago: University of Chicago Press. (originally published in 1776).

Stigler, G. J. 1970. "The Case, if Any, for Economic Education." *Journal of Economic Education*. (Spring).

VanSicle, R. L. 1990. "Learning to Reason With Economics," Working paper on F. A. Walker. "The Tide of Economic Thought." *American Economic Review* (First Series). (January/March 1891).

Walstad, W. B. 1987. "Applying Two-Stage Least Squares," In W. E. Becker and W. B. Walstad, eds. *Econometric Modeling in Economic Education Research*. Boston: Kluwer-Nijhoff Publishing.

_____ and M. Watts. 1990. "The Principles of Economics Textbook: History and Content," In P. Saunders and W. B. Walstad, eds. *The Principles of Economics Course: A Handbook for Instructors*. New York: McGraw-Hill.

_____. 1984. "A Response to Romanish: Ideological Bias in Secondary Economics Textbooks." *Theory and Research in Social Education*. (Winter).

_____. 1985. "Teaching Economics in the Schools: A Review of Survey Findings." *Journal of Economic Education*. (Spring).

Watts, M. 1987. "Ideology, Textbooks, and the Teaching of Economics." *Theory Into Practice*. (Summer).

_____. 1989. "Social Studies Coordinators and a K-12 Program in Economic Education." *Theory and Research in Social Education*. (Winter).

_____ and R. H. Highsmith. 1989. "A Survey of Educational Practices on the International Economy." Working paper.

_____ and R. F. Smith. 1989. "Economics in Literature and Drama." *Journal of Economic Education.* (Summer).

Wentworth, D. R. 1987. "Economic Reasoning: Turning Myth into Reality." *Theory Into Practice.* (Summer).

NINE YEARS OF NATIONAL ECONOMICS EDUCATION: HOW DID WE DO?

John C. Soper

Within the economics education research literature, evidence on the long-term effects of economics education is a scarce commodity. Most evidence is either cross-sectional or longitudinal across a semester or less. Occasionally, a longitudinal study appears with a year's time lapse involved. Longer-term studies are exceptional, however (for example Saunders 1970, 1971, and 1980; and Saunders and Bach 1970).

This is unfortunate, as we possess little information pertaining to the staying power of economics once students have been exposed to instructional programs. In other words, we know little about the retention of economic knowledge after a significant amount of elapsed time between instructional intervention and retesting. The work by Saunders provides us with the best evidence on this, although it is now twenty years old.

It is also difficult to assess the "compound interest" effects of sustained economics education across several different grade levels within a school system, given the dearth of longitudinal studies with a single school system. The study by Buckles and Freeman (1984) provides some information on this topic (the best available), but few researchers carry their analysis beyond a very brief time frame.

The comparative shortage of long-term evidence also affects the economics education movement in another way: we have few benchmarks available to assess the long-term performance of the economics education industry from a macro perspective. Some evidence on the long-term effectiveness of economics education would strengthen its case, particularly vis-à-vis other disciplinary areas in the curriculum.

The comparison samples

An unexploited source of information on the long-term effectiveness of economics education is student performance on the two editions of the *Test of Economic Literacy (TEL)* (Soper 1979; Soper and Walstad 1987). The two editions of the test differ in a number of significant ways, but they also share a great deal in common. Norms for both editions of the *TEL* were established with large, national samples of eleventh- and twelfth-grade student populations. Both editions used large, representative national samples of students "with economics" and "without economics" instruction. Both norm samples contained roughly equivalent breakdowns by sex, census region, and other relevant characteristics. As both test editions focused on high school economics knowledge, both sets of instruments tested over roughly the same body of knowledge.

The similarities (and dissimilarities) between the norm samples of the two editions of the *TEL* are highlighted in Table I. The two samples were collected nine years apart, and both had more than 8,000 student observations. The 1977 sample had 55% of its students with economics instruction, while the 1986 sample had 72% with economics. The earlier sample was collected from 92 high schools in 36 states, whereas the later sample came from 213 schools in 41 states. At least 9 of the schools and 32 states were common to both samples. The gender mix within the two samples was roughly equivalent, with only a 4% differential (more females in the later sample). The 1986 sample contained about 15% more seniors (and therefore, 15% fewer juniors), compared to the 1977 sample. With respect to differences in the distribution of students by type of community, the 1986 sample contained about 15% more students from rural areas, 23% less students from suburban areas, and 11% more students from urban areas. By census region, the 1986 sample had about 6% fewer students from the Northeast, about 4% more students from the North Central region, and about 3% more students from the West. Clearly, the samples are not identical, but one can argue that they are sufficiently similar so that inter-edition comparisons may be fruitful.

Inter-edition item comparability

There is another sense in which the two versions of the *TEL* may be compared. A number of questions were common to both editions of the test. A small number of items were identical on both editions; another small group of questions had "very minor" variations between editions; and a third group had "minor" changes between the 1977 and 1986 editions. Tables II A & B provide a listing of the 49 items which may be compared across the two editions of the *TEL*. These 49 items constitute 53.8% of the original (1977) *TEL*, and 63.6% of the unique items on the revised (1986) edition.

The categorization of questions into "identical", "very minor", and "minor" change groupings is subjective. However, Tables II A & B provide adequate information so that the interested reader can check the author's judgment on this characterization. For the most part, changes between *TEL* editions for various comparable questions mean that the later edition had *shorter* and *more readable* questions, given the greater resources devoted to such details in the second edition. "Identical questions" are just that: no changes are apparent between editions (other than placement order within the test forms). "Very minor" changes mean that (in the author's judgment) very slight changes in wording were made between the two editions. "Minor" changes were a bit more extensive but still judged to be of minimal import. These are the three categories of questions noted in Tables II A & B, and the basis for subsequent comparisons used in this study. Two other categorizations were also made: "Major" changes and "new questions," using the original *TEL* as the basis for judgment. "Major" changes involved fairly significant departures from the original questions, which would make direct comparisons very unreliable. "New" questions involved the complete substitution of new items on the second *TEL* edition. These latter two question categories were omitted from the present study.

From Tables II A & B, one can see that there are 11 "identical" questions, 11 "very minor change" questions, and 27 "minor change" questions in the comparison set. Tables II A & B indicate form and question number for both "old" and "new" versions of the *TEL*, the economic concept tested over, and the P-values (the proportions of students answering given items correctly, or difficulty levels) for students with (Table II-B), and without (Table II-A) economics, by test version. Differences in P-value ("new" and "old") are also indicated, for students with and without economics instruction. The last column in Tables II A & B indicate the nature of the change in each item between editions of the *TEL*.

How did we do?

To begin the analysis of long-term growth in the economics knowledge of U.S. high school students, it is useful to examine the eleven "identical" items which were common to both editions of the test. Table III (based on Tables II A & B) isolate these eleven items and provides P-values (the difficulty levels) for students with, and without economics instruction, by test edition. Table III shows that, after nine years of national economics education programming, the average P-value for the 11 identical *TEL* items fell by 1.5% for students with economics instruction, and by 2.3% for students without economics instruction. These are not large declines, but they are unsettling in the face of significant national efforts to improve student understanding of basic economic concepts.

Table IV provides similar information on the eleven items identified as having "very minor changes" between the two editions of the *TEL*. Students with economics instruction improved the average P-value for the eleven "very minor change" items by 1.5%, whereas students without economics instruction had lower average P-value scores by 1.4%.

Table V completes this level of analysis by separating out the 27 items judged to involve "minor changes" between editions of the *TEL*. For students with economics instruction, the average P-level increased by 0.6, but students without economics instruction had lower P-values, by 3.2.

Tables III-V do not provide evidence of improvement in the level of economic literacy for U.S. high school students. But there may be another way to look at these data from the two editions of the *TEL*.

A look at some aggregate results

On another level of analysis, while the P-value comparisons in Tables II-V provide detailed information on item differences, more useful results may be obtained through aggregation. Table VI presents summary information (again based on Table II A & B), which enables one to make more meaningful comparisons across test editions.

The all-item differences between the two comparable 49-item editions of the *TEL* show very minor changes in the average P-values. These aggregate results are shown in the top section of Table VI. For students with economics instruction, the average score on the 49 common items was 51.9 on the new *TEL*, compared to 51.2 on the old *TEL*. For students without economics instruction, however, students taking the new *TEL* scored only 39.8%, whereas students who took the old *TEL* scored 42.1%. This difference of 2.3 percentage points in mean scores between the "no economics instruction" groups in 1977 and 1986 appears to be small, but it is significant in more than just a statistical sense. One inference from these data is that the general academic ability of the average U.S. high school student has declined. An alternative inference is that the national push for more economics instruction at pre-high school grade levels has not succeeded. This national push has been advocated by the Foundation for Teaching Economics, by the Joint Council on Economic Education, and by Junior Achievement.

If we look at a lower-order aggregation of student scores on the "comparable-item" *TEL*, we can compare scores by "concept cluster" means, using the categorization of Saunders, et al. (1984), into fundamental, microeconomics, macroeconomics, and international economics concept clusters. The second grouping of scores ("By Cluster") in Table VI shows that students in the 1986 norm sample improved their understanding of Fundamental concepts. Students with economics instruction improved by 4.8%, while students without economics improved by 2.8%, compared to equivalent students in the 1977 norm sample. However, for the Microeconomics and Macroeconomics clusters, students in the 1986 norm sample show deterioration, compared to their peers in the 1977 sample. Moreover, this is true for both student groups with and without prior economics instruction. For the final concept cluster, international economics concepts, the results are mixed: students with economics instruction improved slightly (by 1.8%); students without economics instruction, however, worsened their scores slightly (by 1.5%).

The final grouping of comparative aggregate scores in Table VI provides breakdowns on the 49 items by individual economic concept. An additional caveat here is that these breakdowns provide very thin comparative information for some of the concepts, as there are only one or two items in a number of the "concept cells." In such cases, there may be too few items to draw any clear conclusions. But, bearing in mind the foregoing qualification, it appears that the students with economics instruction had improved scores on 50% of the 20 concepts tested. On the other hand, they lost ground on the other 50% of the concepts. For those students without economics instruction, the results by concept are somewhat worse: they improved on only 6 of the 20 concepts tested (30%), and lost ground on the remaining 70% (again, comparing the 1986 norm sample against the 1977 sample).

Conclusions

This brief study depends on two propositions. The first is that the samples of students used to collect norms for the *TEL* in 1977 and again in 1986 were reasonably similar (at least in the sense that they were representative of the high school student populations in the two years). The second is that the 49 items selected for the analysis are truly comparable between editions of the test. On most of the sample characteristics which can be compared, the differences between norm samples do not appear to be large or systematic. We lack the data needed to fully establish the equivalence of the two samples, but there appears to be little reason to argue that they are radically different in some fundamental way. As to the comparability between test editions of the 49 items selected by the author, readers can check the items selected and form their own opinions.

Based on the these assumptions, the resulting analysis suggests the absence of significant gains in student economic literacy between 1977 and 1986. This may be indicative of an overall decline in the academic (or test-taking) ability of the average high school student in the U.S., but we cannot assess that possibility here. If this is the case, however, the nine-year effort to raise student economic literacy has not been able to offset much of the presumed decline in general academic ability or achievement.

If there has been no significant decline in average academic ability, then the economics educator has a long way to go to significantly impact the general level of economic literacy among U.S. high school students.

References

Buckles, S. and V. Freeman. 1984. "A Longitudinal Analysis of a Developmental Economics Education Program." *The Journal of Economic Education.* 15 (Winter), 5-10.

Saunders, P. 1970. "Does High School Economics Have a Lasting Impact?" *The Journal of Economic Education.* 2 (Fall), 39-55.

_____. 1971. "The Lasting Effects of Elementary Economics Courses: Some Preliminary Results." *American Economic Review, Papers and Proceedings.* 61 (May), 242-248.

_____. 1980. "The Lasting Effects of Introductory Economics Courses." *The Journal of Economic Education.* 12 (Winter), 1-14.

_____ & Bach, G. L. 1970. "The Lasting Effects of an Introductory Economics Course: An Exploratory Study." *The Journal of Economic Education.* 1 (Spring), 143-149.

_____ et al. 1984. *A Framework for Teaching the Basic Concepts,* 2nd ed. New York: Joint Council on Economic Education.

Soper, J. C. 1979. *Test of Economic Literacy: Discussion Guide and Rationale.* New York: Joint Council on Economic Education.

_____ and W. B. Walstad. 1987. *Test of Economic Literacy: Second Edition, Examiner's Manual.* New York: Joint Council on Economic Education.

TABLE I

TEL Sample Comparisons

	OLD TEL	NEW TEL	NEW-OLD
Norming dates	May 1977	May 1986	
Sample size	8,660	8,205	-455
No. w/Econ	4,770	5,918	+1148
Percent w/Econ	55	72	+17
No. of schools	92	213	+121
No. of states	36	41	+5

	Econ	None	Total	Econ	None	Total	Econ	None
Form A:	23.99	18.91	21.59	23.33	18.37	22.06	-0.66	-0.54
	2,242	1,817	4,192	3,153	1,082	4,235	+911	-735
Form B:	24.47	20.81	22.89	23.92	18.01	22.13	-0.55	-2.8
	2,528	1,750	4,468	2,765	1,205	3,970	+237	-545
Gender [%]:								
Female	44.2	47.4	45.6	49.1	51.3	49.7	+4.9	+3.9
Male	55.8	52.6	54.4	50.9	48.7	50.3	-4.9	-3.9
Grade Level [%]:								
11th	30.2	61.0	43.3	20.1	52.5	28.0	-10.1	-8.5
12th	69.8	39.0	56.7	79.9	47.5	72.0	+10.1	+8.5
Community [%]:								
Rural	9.0	6.7	8.0	18.5	35.4	22.9	+9.5	+28.7
Suburban	65.4	77.9	70.8	49.3	43.5	47.8	-16.1	-34.4
Urban	22.4	12.6	18.2	32.2	21.1	29.3	+9.8	+8.5
Mixed	3.1	2.8	3.0	0.0	0.0	0.0	-3.1	-2.8
Region [%]:								
Northeast	17.2	32.4	23.9	19.5	14.3	18.0	+2.3	-18.1
South	25.5	29.4	27.2	23.3	34.0	26.3	-2.2	+4.6
North Central	46.3	26.0	37.4	42.0	39.4	41.3	-4.3	+13.4
West	10.9	12.2	11.5	15.2	12.3	14.4	+4.3	+0.1

Source: Soper (1979), Tables 13 & 14; Soper & Walstad (1987), Tables 15 & 16.

TABLE II-A

Common Items, *TEL* First and Second Editions

Without Economics

Question Nos.			TEL	TEL		
Old	New	Concept	Old	New	Dif	Chg[1]
A1	A25	Scarcity	4.8	20.4	15.6	M
A2	B1	Scarcity	40.1	46.6	6.5	M
B1	A3/B3	Scarcity	34.8	30.2	-4.6	M
B2	A4	Oppor. cost/trade-offs	42.6	39.4	-3.2	M
B3	B2	Oppor. cost/trade-offs	38.2	49.5	11.3	M
B4	B5	Productivity	15.2	17.3	2.1	M
B8	A6/B6	Productivity	40.2	42.9	2.7	I
A6	A7/B7	Economic systems	56.5	57.3	0.8	VM
B43	B11	Institutions & incentives	50.3	60.0	9.7	M
B44	B8	Institutions & incentives	53.2	56.3	3.1	I
A5	B10	Institutions & incentives	53.6	56.3	2.7	M
B5	A9/B9	Institutions & incentives	41.2	35.5	-5.7	M
A32	A12	Exch., money & interdep.	55.0	54.7	-0.3	M
B31	B12	Exch., money & interdep.	20.1	18.9	-1.2	I
A12	A10	Markets & prices	46.3	34.0	-12.3	M
B37	A13/B13	Markets & prices	49.4	47.0	-2.4	M
A11	B14	Supply & demand	47.8	36.8	-11.0	M
A14	A15	Supply & demand	52.5	51.8	-0.7	VM
A16	A16	Supply & demand	53.0	50.2	-2.8	I
B11	A14	Supply & demand	57.8	47.7	-10.1	M
B17	B15	Supply & demand	75.9	70.7	-5.2	I
B18	B16	Supply & demand	67.8	50.6	-17.2	M
B21	A17/B17	Supply & demand	25.9	31.6	5.7	VM
A21	B20	Compet. & mkt. structure	18.6	17.2	-1.4	M

[1] Amount of change from 1st edition to 2nd edition: **I** = Identical; **VM** = Very Minor; **M** = Minor

TABLE II-A (Cont.)
Without Economics

Question Nos. Old	New	Concept	TEL Old	TEL New	Dif	Chg[1]
A36	A21/B21	Income distribution	43.8	52.4	8.6	VM
A10	A20	Income distribution	30.4	29.2	-1.2	VM
B36	A21/B21	Income distribution	42.4	52.4	10.0	VM
B6	B22	Income distribution	62.5	40.6	-21.9	M
A18	B24	Role of government	35.9	33.5	-2.4	M
B10	B25	Role of government	36.4	32.2	-4.2	M
A25	B27	Gross national product	53.0	45.9	-7.1	M
B25	A26/B26	Gross national product	59.7	38.8	-20.9	VM
A33	A27	Aggregate supply	33.9	31.6	-2.3	VM
B33	B28	Aggregate supply	33.6	29.1	-4.5	M
B34	B30	Aggregate demand	58.7	53.1	-5.6	VM
B40	A29/B29	Aggregate demand	35.6	28.6	-7.0	M
A27	A30	Unemployment	59.3	53.0	-6.3	I
B29	B31	Unemployment	45.3	49.5	4.2	I
A28	A31	Inflation & deflation	44.7	34.0	-10.7	I
B24	B33	Inflation & deflation	30.0	24.0	-6.0	I
B28	B32	Inflation & deflation	28.9	25.8	-3.1	I
B35	A34/B34	Monetary policy	35.5	28.9	-6.6	VM
A41	A33	Fiscal policy	30.0	30.2	0.2	I
B32	A36	Fiscal policy	44.3	45.3	1.0	M
B38	A37/B37	Fiscal policy	58.8	42.6	-16.2	M
B7	A39	Comp. advantage/barriers	51.3	40.2	-11.1	M
B42	A41/B41	Comp. advantage/barriers	26.8	44.2	17.4	M
B41	B46	Intl. growth & stability	46.0	36.2	-9.8	M
A35	A46	Intl. growth & stability	33.1	30.4	-2.7	VM

Source: Soper (1979), Tables 8 & 9; Soper & Walstad (1987), Tables 10 & 11.

TABLE II-B

Common Items, *TEL* First and Second Editions

With Economics

Question Nos. Old	New	Concept	TEL Old	TEL New	Dif	Chg[1]
A1	A25	Scarcity	20.8	31.9	11.1	M
A2	B1	Scarcity	60.1	72.5	12.4	M
B1	A3/B3	Scarcity	62.1	56.7	-5.4	M
B2	A4	Opportunity cost/trade-offs	52.5	45.2	-7.3	M
B3	B2	Opportunity cost/trade-offs	43.2	54.9	11.7	M
B4	B5	Productivity	28.6	35.8	7.2	M
B8	A6/B6	Productivity	46.4	50.9	4.5	I
A6	A7/B7	Economic systems	70.2	74.5	4.3	VM
B43	B11	Institutions & incentives	52.9	69.3	16.4	M
B44	B8	Institutions & incentives	64.0	72.0	8.0	I
A5	B10	Institutions & incentives	67.2	68.7	1.5	M
B5	A9/B9	Institutions & incentives	45.4	51.4	6.0	M
A32	A12	Exch., money & interdep.	70.5	72.8	2.3	M
B31	B12	Exch., money & interdep.	38.7	33.1	-5.6	I
A12	A10	Markets & prices	59.0	47.8	-11.2	M
B37	A13/B13	Markets & prices	56.8	61.6	4.9	M
A11	B14	Supply & demand	53.9	48.6	-5.3	M
A14	A15	Supply & demand	57.6	62.2	4.6	VM
A16	A16	Supply & demand	63.1	62.2	-0.9	I
B11	A14	Supply & demand	67.4	65.0	-2.4	M
B17	B15	Supply & demand	75.4	76.3	0.9	I
B18	B16	Supply & demand	71.3	65.2	-6.1	M
B21	A17/B17	Supply & demand	37.0	46.5	9.5	VM
A21	B20	Compet. & mkt. structure	30.2	26.4	-3.8	M

[1] Amount of change from 1st edition to 2nd edition: **I** = Identical; **VM** = Very Minor; **M** = Minor

TABLE II-B (Cont.)
With Economics

Question Nos. Old	New	Concept	TEL Old	TEL New	Dif	Chg[1]
A36	A21/B21	Income distribution	54.9	63.9	9.0	VM
A10	A20	Income distribution	40.7	36.5	-4.2	VM
B36	A21/B21	Income distribution	51.1	63.9	12.8	VM
B6	B22	Income distribution	68.5	53.4	-15.1	M
A18	B24	Role of government	50.6	51.6	1.0	M
B10	B25	Role of government	43.4	39.7	-3.7	M
A25	B27	Gross national product	65.6	59.7	-5.9	M
B25	A26/B26	Gross national product	61.4	52.8	-8.6	VM
A33	A27	Aggregate supply	50.9	44.8	-6.1	VM
B33	B28	Aggregate supply	34.6	42.1	7.5	M
B34	B30	Aggregate demand	66.7	70.8	4.1	VM
B40	A29/B29	Aggregate demand	45.4	40.1	-5.3	M
A27	A30	Unemployment	69.3	62.7	-6.6	I
B29	B31	Unemployment	53.1	63.5	10.4	I
A28	A31	Inflation & deflation	53.6	42.4	-11.2	I
B24	B33	Inflation & deflation	45.0	38.3	-6.7	I
B28	B32	Inflation & deflation	37.2	35.5	-1.7	I
B35	A34/B34	Monetary policy	51.5	46.5	-5.0	VM
A41	A33	Fiscal policy	44.5	36.4	-8.1	I
B32	A36	Fiscal policy	53.5	59.0	5.5	M
B38	A37/B37	Fiscal policy	69.1	58.6	-10.5	M
B7	A39	Comp. advantage/barriers	58.9	53.0	-5.9	M
B42	A41/B41	Comp. advantage/barriers	28.6	56.3	27.7	M
B41	B46	Intl. growth & stability	52.3	41.2	-11.1	M
A35	A46	Intl. growth & stability	39.5	35.7	-3.8	VM

Source: Soper (1979), Tables 8 & 9; Soper & Walstad (1987), Tables 10 & 11.

TABLE III

Identical Items, *TEL* First and Second Editions

Question Nos.			TEL, 1st		TEL, 2nd		Dif.1	Dif.2
Old	New	Concept	Econ	None	Econ	None	Econ	None
B8	A6/B6	Productivity	46.4	40.2	50.9	42.9	4.5	2.7
B44	B8	Institutions & incentives	64.0	53.2	72.0	56.3	8.0	3.1
B31	B12	Exchange, money & interdepend.	38.7	20.1	33.1	18.9	-5.6	-1.2
A16	A16	Supply & demand	63.1	53.0	62.2	50.2	-0.9	-2.8
B17	B15	Supply & demand	75.4	75.9	76.3	70.7	0.9	-5.2
A27	A30	Unemployment	69.3	59.3	62.7	53.0	-6.6	-6.3
B29	B31	Unemployment	53.1	45.3	63.5	49.5	10.4	4.2
A28	A31	Inflation & deflation	53.6	44.7	42.4	34.0	-11.2	-10.7
B24	B33	Inflation & deflation	45.0	30.0	38.3	24.0	-6.7	-6.0
B28	B32	Inflation & deflation	37.2	28.9	35.5	25.8	-1.7	-3.1
A41	A33	Fiscal policy	44.5	30.0	36.4	30.2	-8.1	0.2
		AVERAGES	53.7	43.7	52.1	41.4	-1.5	-2.3

Source: Soper (1979), Tables 8 & 9; Soper & Walstad (1987), Tables 10 & 11.

TABLE IV

"Very Minor Change" Items, *TEL* 1st and 2nd Editions

Question Nos.			TEL, 1st		TEL, 2nd		Dif.1	Dif.2
Old	New	Concept	Econ	None	Econ	None	Econ	None
A6	A7/B7	Economic systems	70.2	56.5	74.5	57.3	4.3	0.8
A14	A15	Supply & demand	57.6	52.5	62.2	51.8	4.6	-0.7
B21	A17/B17	Supply & demand	37.0	25.9	46.5	31.6	9.5	5.7
A36	A21/B21	Income distribution	54.9	43.8	63.9	52.4	9.0	8.6
A10	A20	Income distribution	40.7	30.4	36.5	29.2	-4.2	-1.2
B36	A21/B21	Income distribution	51.1	42.4	63.9	52.4	12.8	10.0
B25	A26/B26	Gross national product	61.4	59.7	52.8	38.8	-8.6	-20.9
A33	A27	Aggregate supply	50.9	33.9	44.8	31.6	-6.1	-2.3
B34	B30	Aggregate demand	66.7	58.7	70.8	53.1	4.1	-5.6
B35	A34/B34	Monetary policy	51.5	35.5	46.5	28.9	-5.0	-6.6
A35	A46	International growth & stability	39.5	33.1	35.7	30.4	-3.8	-2.7
		AVERAGES	52.9	42.9	54.4	41.6	1.5	-1.4

Source: Soper (1979), Tables 8 & 9; Soper & Walstad (1987), Tables 10 & 11.

TABLE V

"Minor Change" Items, *TEL* First and Second Editions

Question Nos. Old	New	Concept	TEL, 1st Econ	None	TEL, 2nd Econ	None	Dif.1 Econ	Dif.2 None
A1	A25	Scarcity	20.8	4.8	31.9	20.4	11.1	15.6
A2	B1	Scarcity	60.1	40.1	72.5	46.6	12.4	6.5
B1	A3/B3	Scarcity	62.1	34.8	56.7	30.2	-5.4	-4.6
B2	A4	Opportunity cost/trade-offs	52.5	42.6	45.2	39.4	-7.3	-3.2
B3	B2	Opportunity cost/trade-offs	43.2	38.2	54.9	49.5	11.7	11.3
B4	B5	Productivity	28.6	15.2	35.8	17.3	7.2	2.1
B43	B11	Institutions & incentives	52.9	50.3	69.3	60.0	16.4	9.7
A5	B10	Institutions & incentives	67.2	53.6	68.7	56.3	1.5	2.7
B5	A9/B9	Institutions & incentives	45.4	41.2	51.4	35.5	6.0	-5.7
A32	A12	Exchange, money & interdepend.	70.5	55.0	72.8	54.7	2.3	-0.3
A12	A10	Markets & prices	59.0	46.3	47.8	34.0	-11.2	-12.3
B37	A13/B13	Markets & prices	56.8	49.4	61.6	47.0	4.9	-2.4
A11	B14	Supply & demand	53.9	47.8	48.6	36.8	-5.3	-11.0
B11	A14	Supply & demand	67.4	57.8	65.0	47.7	-2.4	-10.1
B18	B16	Supply & demand	71.3	67.8	65.2	50.6	-6.1	-17.2
A21	B20	Competition & market structure	30.2	18.6	26.4	17.2	-3.8	-1.4
B6	B22	Income distribution	68.5	62.5	53.4	40.6	-15.1	-21.9
A18	B24	Role of government	50.6	35.9	51.6	33.5	1.0	-2.4
B10	B25	Role of government	43.4	36.4	39.7	32.2	-3.7	-4.2
A25	B27	Gross national product	65.6	53.0	59.7	45.9	-5.9	-7.1
B33	B28	Aggregate supply	34.6	33.6	42.1	29.1	7.5	-4.5
B40	A29/B29	Aggregate demand	45.4	35.6	40.1	28.6	-5.3	-7.0
B32	A36	Fiscal policy	53.5	44.3	59.0	45.3	5.5	1.0
B38	A37/B37	Fiscal policy	69.1	58.8	58.6	42.6	-10.5	-16.2
B7	A39	Comparative advantage/barriers	58.9	51.3	53.0	40.2	-5.9	-11.1
B42	A41/B41	Comparative advantage/barriers	28.6	26.8	56.3	44.2	27.7	17.4
B41	B46	International growth & stability	52.3	46.0	41.2	36.2	-11.1	-9.8

| | | AVERAGES | 52.3 | 42.5 | 52.9 | 39.3 | 0.6 | -3.2 |

Source: Soper (1979), Tables 8 & 9; Soper & Walstad (987), Tables 10 & 11.

145

TABLE VI

Summary Comparisons, Old and New *TEL*

	No. of Items	Old TEL Econ	None	New TEL Econ	None	Diff.1 Econ	Diff.2 None
All-Item Averages	49	51.2	42.1	51.9	39.8	0.7	-2.3
By Cluster:							
Fundamental Concepts	14	51.6	39.0	56.4	41.8	4.8	2.8
Microeconomics Concepts	16	55.1	46.6	54.4	42.4	-0.7	-4.2
Macroeconomics Concepts	15	53.4	43.4	50.2	37.4	-3.2	-6.0
Interntl. Growth & Stability Concepts	4	44.8	39.3	46.6	37.8	1.8	-1.5
By Concept:							
Scarcity	3	47.7	26.6	53.7	32.4	6.0	5.8
Opportunity cost/trade-offs	2	47.9	40.4	50.1	44.5	2.2	4.1
Productivity	2	37.5	27.7	43.4	30.1	5.9	2.4
Economic systems	1	70.2	56.5	74.5	57.3	4.3	0.8
Economic institutions & incentives	4	57.4	49.8	65.4	52.0	8.0	2.3
Exchange, money & interdependence	2	54.6	37.6	53.0	36.8	-1.6	-0.8
Markets & prices	2	57.9	47.9	54.7	40.5	-3.2	-7.4
Supply & demand	7	60.8	54.4	60.9	48.5	0.1	-5.9
Competition & market structure	1	30.2	18.6	26.4	17.2	-3.8	-1.4
Income distribution	4	53.8	44.8	54.4	43.6	0.6	-1.2
Market failures	0	0.0	0.0	0.0	0.0	0.0	0.0
Role of government	2	47.0	36.1	45.7	32.9	-1.3	-3.2
Gross national product	2	63.5	56.4	56.3	42.4	-7.2	-14.0
Aggregate supply	2	42.8	33.8	43.5	30.4	0.7	-3.4
Aggregate demand	2	56.1	47.2	55.5	40.9	-0.6	-6.3
Unemployment	2	61.2	52.3	63.1	51.3	1.9	-1.0
Inflation & deflation	3	45.3	34.5	38.7	27.9	-6.6	-6.6
Monetary policy	1	51.5	35.5	46.5	28.9	-5.0	-6.6
Fiscal policy	3	55.7	44.4	51.3	39.4	-4.4	-5.0
Comparative advantage/trade barriers	2	43.8	39.0	54.7	42.2	10.9	3.2
Balance of payments & exchange rates	0	0.0	0.0	0.0	0.0	0.0	0.0
International growth & stability	2	45.9	39.6	38.5	33.3	-7.4	-6.3

ECONOMICS EDUCATION
AND SATISFACTION WITH
FAMILY DECISION MAKING

Marilyn Kourilsky

This study examines whether parents and youngsters can be taught to apply economic reasoning to everyday family decisions and whether such application increases their satisfaction with the decision-making process.

In family decisions, the desire to preserve the group relationship and the multiple consequences of a group decision mean that dissatisfaction with a particular decision outcome (i.e., product choice) may be difficult to separate from disagreement with the decision process (Davis 1976). The fact that participants in family budgetary decisions have long-standing relationships with one another means that both the existence of a financial problem and the process of problem solving, with its expression of conflicting needs, may be viewed as a threat to the stability of those relationships. Expressions of dissatisfaction with a particular decision outcome may therefore result, not from the fact that the choice process was encumbered by the desire to avoid confrontation -- thus lowering the quality of the decision, but from the fact that a high-quality decision was purchased at the cost of considerable conflict -- and this cost, rather than anything about the product itself, resulted in feelings of dissonance.

The multiple consequences of family budgetary decisions -- the fact that a new car purchase may preclude new home furnishings and/or summer camp -- also guarantees a fair amount of dissatisfaction unrelated to product performance. Those individuals deprived of benefits from forgone opportunities may question whether the new car purchase was really necessary, whether it was necessary at this time, or whether the problem the purchase addressed could have been met by spending less money. They may mask their dissatisfaction concerning the disposition of family resources with disappointment about product performance.

147

Why might a family member be dissatisfied with the group decision-making process relative to a particular decision? There are two principal reasons, both of which tend to diminish an individual's sense of economic and psychological autonomy: (1) the costs of the group decision to the family member may not have been sufficiently articulated so that both the family member and the group were aware of what the family member must forgo as a result of the pending solution; and (2) the family member may not have sufficiently participated in the ranking of benefits forgone (i.e., costs) that led to the ultimate decision. It is also possible that a family member may feel uncomfortable with a group decision-making process because the individual may believe that the expression of self-interest is inconsistent with family cohesiveness.

In this study it is proposed that the use of economic reasoning in family budgetary decisions will lead to greater satisfaction with the decision-making process, precisely because the procedural concomitants of cost-benefit analysis tend to enhance the individual's sense of psychological and economic autonomy. While it might also be argued that the use of economic reasoning in family decision making makes for better decision outcomes, the concern in this study was the satisfaction with the decision-making *process itself.*

Economic reasoning: A hierarchical model

Economic reasoning implies the ability explicitly to view decisions in terms of benefits anticipated versus benefits forgone. The nomenclature used to express this way of thinking is cost-benefit analysis. The ultimate cost which accrues from any choice is the value of the benefits you are giving up (i.e., the opportunity cost).

To utilize economic reasoning, one must have at least an intuitive understanding of the concepts of scarcity, alternative uses of resources, and opportunity cost.

The motivation for economic reasoning begins with individuals endeavoring to satisfy their wants. No want can be satisfied without the use of some resource, since there is no human activity which does not use resources. Even the observance of a beautiful sunset requires the use of a resource (at least the time of the person involved) with which something else could be done.

It is axiomatic that the resources available to us are less than the resources required to satisfy all our conceivable wants. This discrepancy between available and required resources is called scarcity. The existence of scarcity implies that choices must be made among alternative uses of resources. Thus, the automatic consequence of scarcity is the necessity to make decisions, and the automatic consequence of decision making is that costs must be borne, or put another way, benefits must be forgone.

Specifically, one can think of economic reasoning in terms of a decision-making hierarchy that integrates scarcity, alternatives, and opportunity cost.

At *level-1* of the hierarchy there is some evidence that scarcity has been identified as a relevant decision-making issue and that relevant scarce resources are explicitly or tacitly identified. For example, in deciding whether to buy a pet, statements such as "Dogs cost a lot of money." "We're not millionaires." "Who is going to walk and bathe the dog?" and "When are they going to do it?" reflect *level-1* thinking.

At *level-2*, specific alternative uses for the identified resources (e.g., money and time) are acknowledged -- i.e., particular benefits of opportunities forgone are recognized. The following statements are examples of *level-2* thinking: "If we buy a dog, we may not be able to play baseball on Saturdays because that's the only day you'll have to wash the dog," and "You may have to give up your paper route in order to wash the dog."

At *level-3* of the hierarchy, the individual is able to identify those alternative uses (for resources) that are realistically within his or her consideration set and then rank them in terms of the anticipated benefits of each. The following represents *level-3* reasoning: "I'd really rather have a dog than a 10-speed bike, but I don't know if the fun of having a dog is worth giving up the money in order to have time to walk it each day; besides, I'm pitcher on my baseball team, and I'd hate not being able to play baseball on Saturday, but that's the only time I'd have to wash the dog. Maybe we ought to buy a dog next year."

What are the economic and psychological concomitants on cost-benefit analysis, and how do these concomitants contribute to increasing the individual's satisfaction with the family decision-making process? The use of cost-benefit analysis promotes the individual's desire for and involvement in the decision-making process based on the extent to which that individual is the bearer or beneficiary of the decision consequences. This means that if a particular budgetary decision would jeopardize a child's chance to go to summer camp, the child will be motivated to point out that fact -- that is, to see that the list of alternative uses for budgetary resources includes the child's desire to go to camp -- and to bring to bear whatever bargaining strategies are at the child's command to assure that this alternative ranks high at the decision stage.

Such involvement with the decision-making activity tends to enhance the individual's satisfaction with the decision-making process because of any one or a combination of the following factors: (1) *articulation* of costs and benefits forgone -- the individual's costs have been well articulated so that both the individual family member must forgo as a result of the pending decision; (2) *participation* in the ranking of benefits forgone -- the family member has been involved in the prioritization of alternative benefits that led to the final decision; and (3) *weighted participation* in the ranking of benefits forgone -- the family member has been involved in the prioritization in proportion to the costs (i.e., benefits forgone) he or she would have individually borne.

Each of the foregoing factors contributes to the individual's sense of economic and psychological autonomy -- the perception that the individual (as opposed to external forces) controls the course of his or her existence.

The use of economic reasoning also favors the maintenance of family accord. When there is a common decision-making framework, a disappointed individual must look not to the supposed hostility of family members who were successful bargainers but to the process by which the decision was effected. Here is a role for economics education. By substituting a process (cost-benefit analysis) legitimized by training and personal experience for a person whose authority is legitimized by tradition or control over resources, it becomes possible to make decisions without the participating individuals being required to jeopardize either the family's authority structure or its affective relationships. So from the point of view of the family's hedonic needs, cost-benefit analysis should be more satisfying than a decision technique which consists in a more or less direct exercise of or assault on authority.

The study to be reported tested the following specific hypotheses with respect to an instructional intervention designed to increase the level of economic reasoning in the family decision-making process:

1. Instructional mediation, economics education, will increase the level of economic reasoning in family budgetary decisions.

2. Instructional mediation, economics education, will increase the level of children's satisfaction with the decision-making process with regard to family budgetary decisions.

3. Instructional mediation, economics education, will increase the parent's level of satisfaction with the decision-making process with regard to family budgetary decisions.

4. There is a correlation between the satisfaction level of children with the decision-making process and the level of economic reasoning manifested in the decision-making process.

5. There is a correlation between the satisfaction level of parents with the decision-making process and the level of economic reasoning manifested in the decision-making process.

6. There is a correlation between the satisfaction level of parents and their children with regard to specific budgetary decisions.

Methodology and results

The subjects included twenty-seven parents (eleven men and sixteen women) and twenty-seven children from San Diego, California. Of the parents, seventeen were married or living with each other, and ten were single. All were from middle class socioeconomic groups. All parents in the program had fifth or sixth grade children who were participants in a classroom, economics education program called *Mini-Society* (Kourilsky 1983). Two parents per school were chosen randomly from a list of all parents who had children participating in the *Mini-Society* program. These parents were invited to attend parent education seminars in economic reasoning on a biweekly basis. Only one parent from among all those who were invited declined to attend the seminar. The replicable instructional sequence for the parents (implemented concurrently with their children's *Mini-Society*) lasted a total of twelve hours over an eight-week period.

The parents and youngsters were pretested and posttested on the level of economic reasoning revealed in their decision-making process and their level of satisfaction with that process. The specific decisions reported were ones which the family had actually encountered and were budgetary in nature.

The first instrument was a *child-parent log*. In the log the parents (with the guidance of their child) discussed in detail the process they utilized to reach a decision that was budgetary in nature. The guidelines included: (1) the alternative considered, along with what they considered the advantages and disadvantages of each; (2) the actual decision; (3) the rationale for the decision; and (4) how the decision was implemented.

The second instrument was a *satisfaction index*, in which children and parents rated their satisfaction with the decision process on a scale of 1 to 4, with 4 equal to "very satisfied," 3 equal to "somewhat satisfied," 2 equal to "somewhat dissatisfied," and 1 equal to "very dissatisfied." Satisfaction was defined as "how happy you were with the decision-making process."

The parents and children were pretested with regard to the level of economic reasoning manifested in child-parent logs of a recent family budgetary decision. They also were individually pre-

152

tested with regard to their level of satisfaction with the decision-making process.

Then a treatment designed to enhance economic reasoning was implemented for eight weeks. Subsequent to instructional intervention the parents and the children were posttested on the variables just described in the context of yet another family budgetary decision.

The level of economic reasoning reflected in parents' logs of both budgetary decisions was evaluated in terms of a hierarchy of economic reasoning by two expert judges on a scale of 0-3. Judges scored each log at the highest level of economic reasoning exhibited. The criteria were as follows:

Level-0: No recognition or use of economic reasoning.

Level-1: Recognition of the existence of scarce resources.

Level-2: Ability to identify specific alternative uses for scarce resources.

Level-3: Ability to identify those alternative uses that are realistically within one's consideration set and prioritize them in terms of anticipated benefits.

Using the Pearson-Product Moment Correlation, the interscore reliability between judges was 91%.

The parent/child interaction program in economics is comprised of five components: (1) the experience itself, (2) post-experience debriefing, (3) derivation of case studies from post-experience debriefings, (4) parent's analysis of and solution to case studies, and (5) resolution of a hypothetical family dilemma. These components employ a novel combination of instructional variables such as behavioral specifications; examples include modeling, rationales, prompting, practice, and feedback.

T-test results indicate that there was a significant increase in level of economic reasoning in family budgetary decisions after experiencing the economics education program. At the time of the pretest, economic reasoning was, approximately, at level-1 -- recognition of the existence of scarce resources. By the time of the posttest the obtained mean score indicates that reasoning had advanced to between levels 2 and 3 (X pre = 1.26; X post = 2.67).

Children's level of satisfaction increased significantly at the posttest period, as suggested by the second study question. (X pre = 1.96; X post = 3.48). This was also true for parent level of satisfaction (Study Question 3) although parents apparently began the program with a slightly higher level of satisfaction toward the decision-making process than did their children. (X pre = 2.37; X post = 3.59).

Pearson product-moment coefficients were computed to ascertain correlational results associated with hypotheses 4 through 6. Findings indicate all relationships were positive and significant ($p \geq .05$ -- two tail tests). With particular respect to our fourth hypothesis, we found a high, positive correlation between children's satisfaction level and level of economic reasoning (.052). Parent satisfaction was also highly correlated with economic reasoning, (.046). Finally, although parent satisfaction was positively correlated with child satisfaction after experiencing the instruction program, it was also highly correlated prior to exposure to the treatment variable (.070 and .072).

Thus, it appears that all major hypotheses were confirmed. Significant pre-post gains were found for economic reasoning and for parent and child satisfaction. Significant positive correlations were produced between economic reasoning and both parent and child level of satisfaction. Parent and child satisfaction was also highly correlated.

Significant differences, in favor of single parents in all cases, were found for each of the three pre-test measures. At the posttest period, however, no differences were found. This result suggests that, prior to instruction, level of satisfaction in both parent and child as well as economic reasoning, was somewhat higher for single-parent families!

Discussion and conclusions

In our model of family decision making, the key variables affecting satisfaction with the process of budgetary decision-making are (1) use of a common decision process (economic reasoning) and (2) participation in that process by those who will bear its consequences. These are not the process variables usually manipulated. When process variables have been incorporated at all in studies of family decision making, they have been variables related to information search: amount or source of information. There has, to be sure, been some interest in the question of relative influence on decision outcomes, but this research has been hampered by its exclusion of children (husband and wife are considered the relevant decision makers) and by its use of hypothetical rather than real dilemmas (See Bernhardt 1974; Davis 1970, 1971). It has also, as Davis points out, been hampered by a hidden agenda -- a search for the single family member who "actually decides" in a particular decision domain -- thus reducing family decision-making to a special case of individual decision-making (Davis 1976).

The present study remedies these defects. The budgetary decision process tested -- cost-benefit analysis -- meets the special needs of families for a common decision-making framework that takes into account the fact of differing individual needs or objectives. Confirmation of the research hypotheses demonstrates success in manipulating level of economic reasoning (hypothesis 1) and lends support to the contention that higher levels of economic reasoning lead to greater satisfaction for individual participants (hypotheses 2, 3, 4, 5), and also increase joint satisfaction (hypothesis 6).

Whereas research on the amount of consumer education has been found to be a weak predictor of consumer behavior (Moschis and Churchill 1978), research on experience-based instruction in economics has consistently shown such mediation to be effective in converting cognitive learning into actual behavior (Kourilsky 1977, 1979, 1981, 1983, 1986, and 1987). The principal thrust of this study was not a test of the efficacy of experience-based instruction in economics. However, the effectiveness of this particular method of instructional intervention proved to be a key ingredient in our ability to test and affirm that the use of economic reasoning in actual decisions increased satisfaction with the decision-making process.

Although earlier studies have focused exclusively on husbands and wives, the present study includes children. Turk and Bell (1972) observe that parents themselves seem to regard the husband-wife dyad as the relevant family decision-making unit. They observe that parent reports tend to discount the influence of children (in contrast to observational measures which confirm their influence). By requiring the participation of children in the logging of decisions, it was ensured that parent reports would include a discussion of the child's role in the decision.

Whereas most studies of family decision making have been laboratory studies using hypothetical dilemmas, in this study subjects reported real decisions. Both Zelditch (1977) and Davis (1976) point out the importance of real versus laboratory decision making, since the former tends to ignore those dimensions which differentiate family decision making from decision making in other types of groups.

The use of real decisions did mean that the kinds of decisions varied considerably: in some cases the alternatives belonged to the same product class but met different needs. In yet others the alternatives belonged to different product classes. In the present research it was contended that the use of cost-benefit analysis would improve satisfaction with decisions of all kinds -- and that particularly in cases where there was disagreement about the meaning of a particular purchase (whether, for example, the purchase of an auto means transportation or ego enhancement) or on spending objectives themselves, the use of cost-benefit analysis would ensure that the benefits forgone for each group member would be considered.

It is interesting that although single-parent families exhibited higher levels of economic reasoning and higher levels of satisfaction with the decision-making process than two-parent families in the pretest, this advantage disappeared in the posttest. It may be that the benefits argued for the use of economic reasoning -- of participation by all the individuals concerned and the fact that everyone uses the same process -- are relative advantages enjoyed by single-parent families regardless of level of economic reasoning. The children in a single-parent family may be treated more like adults -- e.g., they may be more likely to be consulted about expenditures, and better informed about the limitations of family resources.

In sum, this study suggests that parents and youngsters can be taught to apply economic reasoning to everyday family decisions, and that such application increases their satisfaction with the decision-making process.

References

Bernhardt, K. L. 1974. "Husband-Wife Influence in the Purchase Decision Process of Houses." Unpublished doctoral dissertation, University of Michigan.

Davis, H. L. 1970. "Dimensions of Marital Roles in Consumer Decision Making." *Journal of Marketing Research.* 7 (May), 168-177.

_____. 1971. "Measurement of Husband-Wife Influence in Consumer Purchase Decisions." *Journal of Marketing Research.* 8 (August), 305-312.

_____. 1976. "Decision Making Within the Household." *Journal of Consumer Research.* 2 (March), 241-260.

Kourilsky, M. L. 1977. "The Kinder-Economy: A Case Study of Kindergarten Pupils' Acquisition of Economic Concepts." *The Elementary School Journal.* 77:3 (January), 182-191.

_____. 1979. "Optimal Intervention: An Empirical Investigation of the Role of the Teacher in Experience-Based Instruction." *The Journal of Experimental Education.* 47:4 (Summer), 339-345.

_____. 1980. "Predictors of Entrepreneurship in a Simulated Economy." *Journal of Creative Behavior.* 14:3 (Third Quarter), 175-198.

_____. 1981. "Economic Socialization of Children: Attitude Toward the Distribution of Rewards." *Journal of Social Psychology.* 115 (Spring), 45-57.

_____. 1981. "Co-learners Approach to Parent/Child Economic Education: An Empirical Investigation." *NABTE Review.* 8, 44-45.

_____. 1983. *Mini-Society: Experiencing Real-World Economics in the Elementary School Classroom.* Reading, Massachusetts: Addison-Wesley Publishing Company, Inc.

_____ and E. Graff. 1986. "Children's Use of Cost-Benefit Analysis: Developmental or Non-Existent." *Economic Education: Research and Developmental Issues.* Edited by Steve Hodkinson and David Whitehead. Essex, England: Longman Group Ltd., 127-139.

_____ and M. C. Wittrock. 1987. "Verbal and Graphical Strategies in the Teaching of Economics." *Teaching and Teacher Education.* 3:1 (Spring), 1-12.

Moschis, G. P. and G. A. Churchill, Jr. 1978. "Consumer Socialization: A Theoretical and Empirical Analysis." *Journal of Marketing Research.* 15, 599-609.

Sprey, J. 1969. "The Family as a System in Conflict." *Journal of Marriage and the Family.* 31 (November), 699-706.

Turk, J. L. and N. W. Bell. 1972. "Measuring Power in Families," *Journal of Marriage and the Family.* 34 (May), 215-222.

Zelditch, M., Jr. 1971. "Experimental Family Sociology," *Family Problem Solving: A Symposium on Theoretical, Methodological, and Substantive Concerns.* Edited by J. Aldous, T. Condon, R. Hile, M. Strauss, and I. Tallman. Hinsdale, Illinois: Drydan Press, 55-72.

WHY TEACH THE SOCIAL STUDIES:
A LOOK AT THE RATIONALE
FOR INDIVIDUAL DISCIPLINES

George M. Vredeveld

The rationale for teaching and understanding economics is presented by Brenneke (1990), in *An Economy at Risk: The Case for Economics Education*. This brief paper considers these rationales for teaching other social sciences so they can be compared to the rationale for teaching economics. But it is difficult to identify clear statements of rationale for teaching the individual social sciences or the social studies. Although the social studies long have been a significant part of curricular offerings in the elementary and secondary schools, there still is much disagreement about the role they should play.

Parker and Jarolimek (1984) assert that the social studies have fallen into the shadows of competing schools of social concern. To bring them into the limelight, they argue, the critical role of the social studies must be widely understood and firmly asserted. They contend that the fundamental goal of social studies education is to sustain and fulfill the democratic way of life.

A 1979 report (Osborn 1979) of the National Council for the Social Studies (NCSS) presents broader goals. It leads off with the following statement: "The basic goal of social studies education is to prepare young people to be humane, rational, participating citizens in a world that is becoming increasingly interdependent. . . . A commitment to human dignity and rational process are key to the structure of the social studies curriculum." Thus, the NCSS not only calls for an end product (more humane and participating citizens) but also defines the means (rational process) which, they assert, is a critical, questioning and discovering approach to knowledge.

Several goals and rationale for the teaching of social studies are defined in the Social Studies Priorities, Practices and Needs

Project's (SPAN) report (Morrissett 1982). These include better understanding of (1) the nature of the individual, (2) the nature of society, (3) the nature of values, (4) the nature of knowledge, and (5) the nature of learning.

Taken together, the goals presented by NCSS and SPAN are so broad (e.g. the commitment to improve understanding of knowledge, learning, and the rational process) that they do not help distinguish the social studies from many other disciplines. What is distinctive is the social studies' role in promoting humane and participatory citizenship. The social studies play this principal role because they often are the repository of society's values and traditions and perpetuate the beliefs, values, customs, and traditions of a society in their transmission of knowledge.

Although the establishment of a clear rationale would seem to be basic to social studies education, few curricula and many of the popular social science textbooks fail to discuss why the social studies should be taught. And when the rationale is presented, there seems to be considerable disagreement. This lack of unanimity may simply be reflective of the different goals and rationale of the individual disciplines that underlie the social studies. We will consider the rationale for teaching each of the social sciences in the following paragraphs in order to gain more information about similarities and special differences that may exist among them.

Geography

Geographers have probably done more work than most social scientists in identifying the rationale for their discipline than other social scientists. Salter (1989) states that one of life's basic necessities is to have knowledge of the world. Geography, he says, has the capacity to make sense out of the landscapes of life and the individual's role in shaping society by interacting with the environment. Salter contends that geography serves social studies best when it helps people to understand why things happen where and when they did, why people migrate, and why some races have such tumultuous history. Anderson (1986) emphasizes the behavioral aspects of geography even more. He feels students should understand that the abilities and skills necessary for the development of the world's environment will continue to vary significantly. His greatest emphasis is not on natural resources, but the human skill, financial capital, and motivation for people to exploit their resources. He states that instructors should stress that most, if not all, environments are not natural, but cultural.

Sociology

Sociology's goal is two-fold -- to create a better understanding of society (i.e., the search for theoretical universals in human behavior) and to facilitate personal improvement and social adjustment. While many sociologists feel it is important to understand the complex choices people must make, they also are eager to *prescribe* a way by which to change the world and make it better. Accordingly, the rationale for teaching sociology seems to be that students gain greater insight into their own troubles by studying public issues through the sociological perspective. Perhaps Gray (1989) is representative of sociologists when he states that " . . . sociology's agenda is so ambitious and its findings require a tolerance for ambiguity, it is difficult to summarize the entire discipline in a format which could readily find its way into the high school curriculum. However, . . . it is desirable to include modules or units illustrating the sociological perspective and fostering an attitude of critical awareness."

Anthropology

In her NCSS essay, White (1989) states "The central goal of anthropologists is to explain why groups of people are different from each other, to explain why they have different physical characteristics, speak different languages, use different technologies, and why they think, believe, and act so differently." She contends that when we learn more about others, we learn more about ourselves. Anthropologists see their role as the development of a holistic study of man, a broad view of human behavior, or even a holding company of ideas and theories shared with many and different disciplines. Anthropologists have done little work in building a rationale for teaching anthropology at the elementary and secondary level.

Psychology

Psychologists have not agreed about why psychology should be taught. On one side are psychologists who feel the goal should be the development of scientific knowledge and the scientific method. On the other side are those who emphasize a personal problem approach. The disagreement reflects different views of the nature of psychology. One group sees psychology as a natural science; a second group sees it as a social science; while still others see it as a bridge between the natural and social sciences. Kasschau and Wertheimer (1974) represent the "bridge" viewpoint. They feel it is essential for people to develop better self-knowledge and improve themselves, and they argue that personal adjustment and mental hygiene are the two most important objectives in teaching psychology. They further state that in order to provide a balanced overview of psychology one must teach it as a scientific discipline but then help students to see the relevance of psychological knowledge in their own lives and in articulating their own feelings and patterns of social interaction. Although the two viewpoints can be linked, the division is clear. One school promotes better understanding of the scientific method; the other school contends that psychology should be taught so students can better understand themselves.

Political science

Political scientists have developed rather broad goals and multiple rationales. The basic purpose of teaching government and politics, according to one group, is to discover why humans think, organize and act politically. This is essential, they argue, because all of life is affected by politics. To accomplish this discovery, political science should transmit to students a knowledge of the realities of political life and the cultural ideas of American democracy. Also, students should develop a capacity to think critically about political issues. In this vein, Becker (1968) emphasizes that political science should help young people live creatively and cooperatively.

Furthermore, political scientists believe it is essential for young people to have knowledge about formal government institutions and legal structures, both in the United States and abroad.

Collier (1966) emphasizes the role that political science should play in understanding fundamental processes and relationships beyond the leaning of isolated facts.

History

McNeil (1989) maintains that history should be taught because students need to realize that they share the earth with people whose beliefs and actions are different from their own. However, this succinct statement is only one of many offered by historians. Chilcoat (1985) reviewed 638 articles and five popular magazines, and came up with ten dominant rationales for teaching history. In addition, he lists an additional 251 rationales, but claims that ten dominate the rest. They are briefly described as follows: The *historical method* seeks to develop the process of thinking through the means of generalized method. *Historical mindedness and perspective* refers to the development of a frame of reference to be applied to personal situations and contemporary events that will give an individual a more balanced view of life. *Historical knowledge* refers to the development of a supply of acquired facts that distinguishes one as an educated and a thinking person. The *study of man* develops an understanding of the unique nature of men and women and acquaints people with their heritage as human beings.

Citizenship training develops useful and well-informed citizenship, including an appreciation for patriotic ideals and beliefs and encouragement of community participation. The *understanding of society* serves as a guide to analyze social action and society. *Self-knowledge and self-awareness* refer to the development within students of a consciousness of being and an awareness of knowing themselves, their purposes, and their goals in the task of acquiring a sense of self. *Cultural heritage* is to transmit traditions, customs, and values as a process of socialization. *Multi-ethnic and minority study* develops an understanding of the students own heritage and that of others so as to better function in a pluralistic society. The *development of a system of values* contains three different approaches. The first is to develop within students ways to behave that are consistent with norms and morals of American society. The second is to acquaint students with the various value

165

systems that pervade American society, and the third approach is to provide students with opportunities to examine, analyze, understand, and choose their own personal value systems.

Such a long list indicates that historians have not reached a consensus about why history should be taught. And many of the rationales have not been developed fully in regard to actual implementation in the classroom. Chilcoat argues that the teaching of history will not be improved until teachers have a clear notion of what they are specifically trying to do and why they are trying to do it.

Conclusions

There is no real consensus on why the social science disciplines should be taught. Each discipline has gone about its work without much regard to the others. If there is a distinguishable central theme, it is that students should understand more about the society in which they live so that they can become better citizens.

Given its strong commitment to develop "better citizens," economics shares this basic underlying theme. Its rationale also has common ground with those rationales that stress the importance of developing the scientific method and critical thinking.

However, the economist's emphasis on the importance of seeking with those theoretical universals and generalizations that will assist in analyzing, understanding, and predicting human behavior has not been widely adopted by other social scientists. And the rationales that are normative or emphasize the accumulation of information about people, beliefs, and institutions have not been widely adopted by economists.

References

Anderson, Randall C. 1986. "Geography as a Behavioral Study in the Social Sciences." *Social Education.* 50, 136.

Baum, Cynthia G. and Ira S. Cohen. 1989. "Psychology and the Social Science Curriculum." *Charting a Course: Social Studies for the 21st Century.* Washington, D.C.: National Commission on Social Studies in the Schools, 65-69.

Becker, James M. 1968. *An Examination of Objectives, Needs and Priorities in International Education in U.S. Secondary and Elementary Schools.* New York: Foreign Policy Association, 127.

Bohannan, Paul. 1966. *Anthropology.* Publication #106 of the Social Science Education Consortium, Purdue University, Lafayette, Indiana.

Brenneke, Judith Staley. 1991. *An Economy at Risk: The Case for Economics Education.* Atlanta, Georgia: Society of Economics Educators.

Brody, Richard A. 1989. "Why Study Politics?" *Charting a Course: Social Studies for the 21st Century.* Washington, D.C.: National Commission on Social Studies in the Schools, 59-63.

Chilcoat, George W. 1985. *A Study of the Rationales and Their Implications for Studying American History in the Secondary Schools: A Review of the Literature 1960 to 1980.* Paper presented at the Annual Meeting of the American Educational Research Association, Chicago, March 1985.

Collier, David. 1966. *The Political System.* Publication #103 of the Social Science Education Consortium, Purdue University, Lafayette, Indiana.

Gray, Paul S. 1989. "Sociology." *Charting a Course: Social Studies for the 21st Century*. Washington, D.C.: National Commission on Social Studies in the Schools, 71-75.

Kasschau, Richard A. and Michael Wertheimer. 1974. *Teaching Psychology in Secondary Schools*. Washington D. C.: American Psychological Association, 72.

Kingston, Paul W. and Clifford T. Bennett. 1986. "Improving High School Social Studies: Advice from the Colleges." *Theory and Research in Social Education*. XIV:1, pp. 35-49.

Littleford, Michael S. 1973. "Teaching Anthropological Processes and Perspectives." *The Secondary School High School Journal*. 56:4, 207-216.

McNeill, William H. 1989. "World History." *Charting a Course: Social Studies for the 21st Century*. Washington, D.C.: National Commission on Social Studies in the Schools, 53-58.

Morrissett, I., ed. 1982. *Social Studies in the 1980s -- A Report of Project SPAN*. Alexandria, Virginia: Association for Supervision and Curriculum Development.

Osborn, Richard, et. al. 1970. "Revision of the NCSS Social Studies Curriculum Guidelines." *Social Education*. (April), 261-273.

Parker, Walter and John Jarolimek. 1984. "Citizenship and the Critical Role of the Social Studies." *NCSS Bulletin* (no. 72). Boulder, Colorado: ERIC Clearinghouse for Social Studies/ Social Science Education Consortium, National Council for the Social Studies.

Pietrofesa, John J. 1969. "Psychology in the High School: A Course Designed to Increase Self-Understanding." *Journal of Secondary Education*. 44:2, 51-54.

Ross, Robert J. 1972. *A Conceptual Program for High School Psychology in the Schools*. 9:4, 418-422.

Salter, Christopher. 1989. "Geography." *Charting a Course: Social Studies for the 21st Century.* Washington, D.C.: National Commission on Social Studies in the Schools, 43-47.

Sprinthall, Norman A. 1980. "Psychology for Secondary Schools: The Saber-Tooth Curriculum Revisited?" *American Psychologist.* 35:4, 336-347.

Stephens, James Russel. 1987. *Methodology in Pre-Collegiate Anthropology: A Secondary School Approach.* Dissertation, 182.

White, Jane J. 1989. "Anthropology." *Charting a Course: Social Studies for the 21st Century.* Washington, D.C.: National Commission on Social Studies in the Schools, 31-36.

Zunino, Natalia. 1974. "The Teaching of Psychology in American High Schools: What's Happening?" *Social Education.* 38:3, 256-259.

A CRITIQUE OF
AN ECONOMY AT RISK

Michael A. MacDowell

I am not a good choice as the discussant for these papers. It is difficult for me to be critical because I have spent all but the last two years of my professional life defending, extolling the virtues of, and otherwise espousing the importance of economics education. Hence, I will not critique what is said in these papers, which is quite good. Rather I am interested in what is not said. These papers do not alert the reader to the serious dilemma faced by economics education, nor do they call for immediate action on the part of those who could most help the situation.

On January 5 (1991) Nobel Prize winning physicist Dr. Leon Lederman released a report to the press and his colleagues in the 130,000 member American Association for the Advancement of Sciences (AAAS) (*New York Times* 1991). The report is a scathing indictment of national priorities. Based on his interview of 250 scientists at fifty universities, Lederman paints a picture of a science research and science education program that is "beset by flagging morale, diminishing expectations, and constricting horizons." The reason, according to Professor Lederman, is that science education and research funding has increased by only twenty percent, in real terms, between 1968 and 1990, while the number of Ph.D.'s has doubled in that period. The answer? Double the science budget for research and science education in the next two years, and then plan on a eight to ten percent increase thereafter. His report was soundly endorsed by the AAAS which is actively lobbying for these funds.

Professor Lederman readily admits that he may be sending a self-serving message. He believes the risk of doing so, however, far outweighs the risk of not making the case for significantly increased funding of education and research.

Professor Lederman's findings are relevant here for only one reason -- to show how poorly economics education is funded. While money for science research and education increased twenty percent from 1968 to 1990, funds for economics education programs, as measured by the budget of the national Joint Council on Economic Education and its affiliates, increased only ten percent in the same period. Starting with an infinitely smaller base, funds for economics education grew much slower than those for science. In real dollars, science education and research have suffered a one percent growth rate during the past twenty years. Funds available for economics education, however, *declined* four to five percent. During the same twenty-two year period, the number of high school students taking science in schools declined six percent, while the number of high school students taking economics has *increased* substantially as Soper points out. (A similar increase in economics enrollment is reported in a forthcoming *Journal of Economic Literature* paper by William Walstad (1991). He suggests enrollment has increased by approximately nine percent between the mid-1970s and late-1980s. Walstad estimates that twenty-nine percent of the high school graduates are now enrolled in economics.) Put simply, we have fewer dollars and more students.

There is further evidence of the relative lack of support for economics education:

- Grants for economics education from the National Science Foundation, previously one of the mainstays of innovative pre-college economics education, has all but disappeared.

- Support for teacher education in economics in the nation's two largest states, California and New York, was one of the first areas to be entirely cut when the recession woes hit home.

- Interest in the subject matter, as measured by economics inclusion in the revised National Assessment of Education Progress, is also low. Economics is number seven among the ten areas to be reviewed on a periodic basis by The National Assessment of Educational Progress. Currently *no* funds are provided for any of the named assessment areas and the long-run prognosis from Washington is that funds will be provided for *only* the first five. Hence, once again, there will be no bench mark data upon which to measure student economic literacy.

With increased enrollments, due primarily to new state mandates, on one hand, and diminished real dollars available for quality economics education programs, on the other, there can be little doubt as to why we have seen no significant gains in high school students' economic knowledge between 1977 and 1986 as reported by Soper. Where is the blame to lie? There is plenty enough to go around, but in its broadest sense the problem lies with economists themselves. While Lederman and thousands of his colleagues in the hard sciences lobby tirelessly for education and research support for their disciplines, economists remain politely aloof when it comes to support for economics education. In some instances they actually discourage support for the field.

Rushing's paper is a short one, as it must be, because few economists of import have had much to say in support of pre-college economics. No AEA president has discussed the topic in a presidential address. Any allegiance to economics education by the economists Rushing cites can mostly be explained by circumstance: Stein and Silk are journalists and their economics education statements appear in the popular press, far away from the controversy or complacency that might erupt if such statements were made to the profession. Heyne has a best-selling textbook. More economics education generates more royalties. Cyert's *Journal of Economic Education* article was given at the annual meeting of the Joint Council, so he was speaking to friends in court. This is not to demean the support of these economists nor other leaders in the profession who have donated untold hours of volunteer time to economics education programs. It does suggest that public advocacy for economics education on the part of the vast majority of economists, and professional associations of economists has been almost nonexistent.

What Rushing does not cite are the disparaging comments made about economics education by Nobel Laureate Friedman (unless, of course, he is speaking about his own economics educational TV series), Stigler (1970) and others.

The American Economic Association's leadership has certainly had the occasion to speak on the need for increased support of economics education. In 1961 the National Task Force on Economic Education, co-chaired by G. L. Bach (1961) and Paul Samuelson, called for increased participation in economics education programs by economists. They also requested that economists become more involved in promoting and supporting economics instruction in the schools. In the thirty years since the Task Force report, the AEA has swept advocacy for economics education aside. Phil Saunders states it well in his paper based on the review of minutes of the AEA from 1944 through 1990:

The story . . . is one of the evolution of an increasingly activist and project-oriented AEA policy that has involved a significant number of professional economists in a wide variety of activities. None of these activities [however] have committed the Association, as such, to questions on what to teach or how to teach it at any level of economics instruction.

Rushing's cautioned conclusions about economist's advocacy for economics education are also telling. "I think we have discovered at least the embryo of what we hoped would be there. Some who are among the distinguished in the profession have indeed nodded to the importance of economics education." This is hardly a ringing endorsement. It seems that economists have chosen to eschew responsibility for enhancing the quality and quantity of their own discipline at the pre-college level, while their colleagues in the hard sciences, as well as many of the social sciences such as geography, speak eloquently, and lobby effectively, for school programs in their disciplines.

Economists should be involved in the support of economics education for reasons that transcend funding. Quite frankly, what often passes for economics education in the schools today cannot often be classified as economics or education. Frustrated by lack of progress in the field, and buttressed by a desire to "help our schools," business, foundations, and individuals are spending vast sums of private money on programs which fit the economics education rubric, yet which produce students who know no more economics than when they entered the program. O'Neill did a fine job of tracing quotes from industry leaders about the need for economics education. The fact of the matter is, however, that these business leaders, and much more important their lieuten-

174

ants, are *easily* swayed by programs that promise economic literacy, but do not deliver. These efforts could easily be redirected, however, if the profession would take a stand on what constitutes a minimal economics education program, and what does not.

To return to the task at hand, any paper which calls for more quality economics education is a good one, and Brenneke's is no exception. Similarly, O'Neill and Rushing have done their best to find quotable statements from economists and business leaders alike, supporting economics education. But the conclusion the reader will reach after completing these papers is that economics education is alive and well, and it just needs a little shove. This is simply not the case. The field has lost funding and important friends and cannot continue to do so if it is to remain viable. Our colleagues in the sciences and other social sciences are seeing to it that funds are available so that their subjects are taught by trained teachers. Economists are not. Further, by their disinterest economists are encouraging inferior programs to substitute for viable ones in the nation's schools.

What can be done? Clearly the profession needs to be reminded that quality economics education can occur in the nation's schools. *An Economy at Risk: Does Anyone Care?* and Walstad's article begin this process. But that is not enough. It is time that the profession once again take a leadership role in economics education as it did thirty years ago when it established the National Task Force on Economic Education. A new task force should be established and will hopefully include Nobel laureates and former AEA presidents. The Second National Task Force on Economic Education should undertake the following tasks:

- Review, and amend if necessary, the *Framework for Teaching Economics*, published by the Joint Council on Economic Education and written by the few leading economics education activists in the profession. The *Framework* first appeared in 1977 and was updated in 1984. It outlines the basic economic concepts, or understandings, with which a student should be familiar upon graduation from high school.

175

- Based upon the new *Framework*, the Task Force should review the most popular high school textbooks and critique them for content accuracy and for adherence to the basic principles of economics. Importantly, the Task Force should identify the inadequacies within existing high school textbooks, and if they are found wanting, make suggestions for revisions.

- The Task Force should also examine the most popular economics education programs and determine which are most effective and efficient in producing economically literate high school graduates.

- Like the American Mathematical Association has recently done for pre-college math instruction, the Task Force should agree upon the appropriate tools for assessing economic knowledge (see Chira 1991). Ideally, the Task Force would also outline the parameters for measuring the behavioral outcomes associated with economics education literacy.

The findings of the Task Force should be presented at the annual meetings of the AEA, and endorsed by the AEA president in his or her annual address. Following the report, Task Force members should join with other distinguished economists in disseminating the findings and promoting the action agenda developed by the Task Force. This three-year effort should be coordinated by the AEA Committee on Economic Education.

In the final analysis, economists must bring the case for real economics education to decision makers in the public and private sectors and thereby generate the support that this important field deserves. Without that support economics education will, to borrow from a physicist, "be beset by flagging morale, diminishing expectations, and constricting horizons."

References

1991. "Nobel Physicist Raises Alarm on U.S. Science." *New York Times*. (5 January), 16.

Bach, G. L. 1961. "Economics in the High Schools: The Responsibility of the Profession." *American Economic Review*. (May).

Chira, Susan. 1991. "The Big Test: How to Translate Talk About School Reform into Action?" *New York Times*. (24 March), E1 and 4.

Stigler, George. 1970. "The Case, If Any, for Economic Literacy." *Journal of Economic Education*. (Spring), 77-84.

Walstad, William B. "Economics Instruction in the Schools: A Thirty Year Perspective." Manuscript for publication in *Journal of Economic Literature*.

COMMENTS ON "AN ECONOMY AT RISK: DOES ANYONE CARE?"

David D. Ramsey

I am currently a co-chair on a dissertation committee for one of our Doctor of Arts students. The purpose of his dissertation is to design an economics course to be taught to fourth-year (equivalent to the tenth grade in the United States) secondary-school students in Zaire. To construct and implement such a course requires that a case for economics education be established. Being familiar with the conventional wisdom that provided support for economics education, I was disappointed that my student was unable to go much beyond that. In particular, he was not successful in finding any empirical support for the conventional wisdom. So it was with great pleasure and anticipation that I accepted an invitation to discuss papers at a session devoted exclusively to the case for economics education in the hopes that the apparent void uncovered by my graduate student would be filled.

Before discussing the four papers which I have been assigned, let me give you my perspective on how these papers relate to each other and to the overall theme of this session. Brenneke's paper sets the tone of the series and serves as a general position paper for the topic. She gives an excellent presentation of the general case for economics education based on standard economic analysis. The papers by Rushing and O'Neill provide academic and business support for the case made by Brenneke, based on the pronouncements of an impressive list of academic economists and business leaders. Soper's paper represents an attempt to provide an empirical test of how well economics education is achieving the goals established by Brenneke. Soper's approach is typical of how others have approached this problem. The authors are to be congratulated on how well the papers cover the theme of the session and, especially, for how well integrated the papers are.

At one level, the papers accomplish well their intended goals. At another level, the papers raise important questions and issues that are not so well addressed. This will leave readers wishing that the authors had tried to answer some of the difficult issues they themselves raised rather than devoting so much attention to familiar territory. Admittedly, the unexplored issues provide us with substantial challenges, but I think it is time to start addressing these issues to develop a firmer basis on which to evaluate economics education. The thrust of my discussion of these papers is to encourage the authors to consider how to resolve some of these difficult problems. My comments are organized according to issues, rather than by author, since several authors address each of the identified issues.

It is common to characterize economics education as a public good as Brenneke does in her paper; see also McKenzie (1977). A more appropriate description of economics education is that it is capable of generating an externality. To generate an externality, however, an individual must engage in some private action. The fact that a person has taken some economics courses does not affect anyone else until that person acts. In the public domain, the individual must decide to vote or speak out on issues. Contrary to many political scientists, who concentrate on why people *don't* vote, economists are surprised that people *do* vote, if the decision to vote is made entirely on a rational cost-benefit basis. On the one hand, we educate students to be better voters. On the other hand, we provide them with economic logic that discourages them from using that knowledge in the public arena. Brenneke herself points out that it is the private benefits that persuade individuals to learn economics. For a contrary view, note the comments by Herbert Stein quoted in Rushing's paper. Simply stating that economics education is a public good and therefore is deserving of public and private support is not enough. We must also specify a mechanism whereby individuals will have an incentive to put that education to use and generate the positive externalities that economics educators identify.

In Brenneke's discussion of positive and normative economics she defines, as so many others do, positive economics as "*what is.*" This definition minimizes the science of economics. A better way to make a distinction between positive and normative is to define them as testable and non-testable. This would emphasize the predictive content of economics and would be less constraining in the eyes of students. Although Brenneke proceeds with a discussion of this predictive nature and the testability of positive concepts, this could be better emphasized with a different definition.

Brenneke states that economics education leads individuals to become better decision makers in both their private and public decisions. She also states "that economics teaches best the rational thinking process," a point also made by Stigler (1970). The ways in which students are better decision makers are usually not specified. In particular, what are the efficiency gains, and how can they be measured? These are the important and unanswered questions. Rather than measuring efficiency gains, we resort to test scores on examinations, assuming that higher test scores will generate higher efficiency gains. This is the approach that Soper followed in his paper and that others before him have also adopted. Brenneke states "this [test scores] does not directly tell us how economics will influence the behavior of these students as producers, consumers, or as voting citizens." She also states that there is no "solid evidence that an understanding of economics will improve an individual's societal or citizenship role." I would add that there is also no evidence about how private decisions are improved by economics education. What is needed is hard evidence on the benefits and costs of economics education to properly evaluate it. Perhaps some economic games could be devised to test the relative decision-making capabilities of students with and without economics education. O'Neill also asks for hard evidence when he lists questions that potential financial supporters of economics education may ask. One of those questions is: "What returns have we received from our investment in economics education?" Soper too recognizes the problem when he states that "evidence on the long-term effects of economics education is a scarce commodity."

On the surface, Rushing's paper offers evidence of support for economics education by prominent economists. Rushing states:

> I think what we have discovered is at least the embryo of what we hoped would be there. Some who are among the distinguished in the profession have indeed nodded to the importance of economics education.

I don't consider this a ringing endorsement of economics education. This damning by faint praise suggests that professional support and research by economists must be evaluated within the framework of the reward structure faced by academic economists, and the means by which collective decisions on the goals of economics education can be determined. Economics education does not have the same stature within economics as mathematics education does within mathematics. Related to this issue is the special-interest support that establishes goals for economics education that a more objective group would not choose.

Soper is clearly disappointed in his finding that the test score on a standardized subset of questions on the *Test of Economic Literacy* (1987) by high school students in 1986 was only seven-tenths of a percentage point higher than the test score by high school students in 1977. His comparison of the two samples, as well as the basis for comparison, is valid. He does his best to present the results in a way that most favorably reflects the test score outcomes of the economics education delivery system. I wonder if the results on student attitudes toward economics would be similar. Soper suggests that the test data on high school students with no economics support the view that the general academic ability of students has declined between 1977 and 1986 because of the 2.3 percentage-point decline in their test scores. If this is the case, then how well prepared are students to effectively learn economics? Is it efficient to allocate educational resources to the teaching of specialties such as economics at the expense of more basic skills such as reading and mathematics?

As disappointed as Soper is about his findings, they are made to seem worse by attempting to suggest that the slight increase in test scores from 1977 to 1986 can be interpreted as evidence of the long-term effects of economics education on high school students. The conclusion that I would draw from the data presented is that the stock of economics knowledge by high school students with an economics course in 1986 is slightly higher and is distributed differently across concepts compared to that of 1977 high school students with an economics course. I don't think any conclusion can be made from this study about the long-term effects of economics education on high school students. To do this would require a carefully constructed longitudinal study of high school students.

Soper's findings do suggest some long-term conclusions about the economics education delivery system. One, even if high school student quality was the same in the two years, economics education made it possible for high school students to achieve a slightly higher average test score in 1986 compared to 1977. And, if student quality deteriorated as suggested by Soper, then economics educators have improved more than is reflected in the test scores. There is another sense in which long-term improvements in economics education may have been achieved, and that is reflected in the greater percentage of high school students with economics in 1986 compared to 1977. Economics test scores of randomly selected high school students in 1986 would be higher than the test scores of randomly selected high school students in 1977. Greater coverage of students represents a long-term improvement in economics education, especially if externalities are generated as a result.

These papers reflect accurately the current state of economics education in the primary and secondary school system. I hope the authors will now turn their attention to some of the issues raised and try to find concrete evidence to support the rationale offered for economics education.

References

McKenzie, Richard B. 1977. "Where is the Economics in Economic Education?" *The Journal of Economic Education.* (Fall), 5-13.

Stigler, George J. 1970. "The Case, if Any, for Economic Literacy." *The Journal of Economic Education.* (Spring), 77-84.

Soper, John C. and W. B. Walstad. 1987. *Test of Economic Literacy.* New York: Joint Council on Economic Education.

ABOUT THE CONTRIBUTORS

JUDITH STALEY BRENNEKE is Managing Director of the education consulting firm, Rational Education Associates, and Lecturer in economics at John Carroll University, Cleveland, Ohio.

STEPHEN BUCKLES is President of the Joint Council on Economic Education, New York, New York.

CALVIN A. KENT is Administrator of the Energy Information Administration, United States Department of Energy and is on leave from Baylor University, Waco, Texas.

MARILYN KOURILSKY is Professor of Education at the University of California - Los Angeles, President and Executive Director of the California Council on Economic Education, and Director of the UCLA Center on Economic Education. This paper is an adaptation of a research endeavor on cost-benefit analysis in family decision making conducted in association with Trudy Murray.

MICHAEL A. MACDOWELL is Vice President for External Affairs at Hartwick College, Oneonta, New York, where he also teaches economics. He is a Director of the Calvin K. Kazanjian Economics Foundation and served as President of the Joint Council on Economic Education from 1977-1989. This paper was first presented at the Eastern Economic Association meetings, March 15, 1991.

JAMES B. O'NEILL is Professor of Economics and President of the Delaware Council on Economic Education at the University of Delaware, Newark, Delaware.

DAVID D. RAMSEY is Professor of Economics at Illinois State University, Normal, Illinois. This paper was first presented at the Eastern Economic Association meetings, March 15, 1991.

FRANCIS W. RUSHING is Professor of Economics and Holder of the Bernard B. and Eugenia A. Ramsey Chair of Private Enterprise at Georgia State University, Atlanta, Georgia.

PHILLIP SAUNDERS is Professor of Economics and Director of the Center for Economic Education at Indiana University, Bloomington, Indiana.

JOHN C. SOPER is Professor of Economics at John Carroll University, Cleveland, Ohio. He was the author of the original *Test of Economic Literacy* (1979) and coauthor (with William Walstad) of the second edition (1987).

GEORGE M. VREDEVELD is Professor of Economics at the University of Cincinnati and Director of the Greater Cincinnati Center for Economic Education, Cincinnati, Ohio.

MICHAEL WATTS is Associate Professor of Economics and Director of the Center for Economic Education at Purdue University, West Lafayette, Indiana.

DENNIS WEIDENAAR is Dean of the Krannert School of Management, Purdue University, West Lafayette, Indiana.